VOGUE KNITTING

BABY BLANKETS TWO

VOGUE KNITTING

BABY BLANKETS TWO

SIXTH&SPRING BOOKS
NEW YORK

SIXTH&SPRING BOOKS
233 Spring Street
New York, New York 10013

Copyright© 2004 by Sixth&Spring Books
All rights reserved including the right of reproduction
in whole or in part in any form.

Library of Congress Cataloging-in-Publication Data

Vogue knitting baby blankets two.--1st ed.
    p. cm. -- (Vogue knitting on the go!)
    ISBN 1-931543-43-7
    1. Knitting--Patterns. 2. Blankets. I. Title: Baby blankets two. II.
Title: Vogue knitting baby blankets 2. III. Vogue knitting international.
IV. Series.

    TT825 .V5828 2004
    746.43'20437--dc21   2003054215

Manufactured in China

1 3 5 7 9 10 8 6 4 2

First Edition

TABLE OF CONTENTS

INTRODUCTION

There's no better way to welcome a newborn into this world than with a cuddly soft baby blanket stitched with care. It is not only a way to show your affection or an excuse to knit; often it is also a child's first material possession, security blanket, and exposure to the love of a person close to him or her. And these days, when time is of the essence, baby blankets are quick and portable projects that mean even more to the people who make them and the tykes who enjoy them. Wherever you are—at home or on the road— a few rows here and there add up swiftly, and voilà! A blanket is ready to be wrapped around your little one.

But you don't have to be a knitter on the move to appreciate and enjoy this diverse collection of patterns; you just have to love knitting, babies, or both! Animal enthusiasts will reach for the sweet Sheep Motif blanket, while color lovers will gravitate towards the Southwest-tinged Crazy Stripes blanket. Meanwhile knitters with a more subdued aesthetic will take a look at the delicate Shell Stitch blanket or Entrelac Throw—styles which manage to be classic and contemporary at the same time. Whether you already have something in mind or don't know where to start, one (or even more) of these projects will have you clicking your needles as quickly as you can cast on. And, as babies develop, so do their tastes and styles, which means that whatever blanket you don't get to make today you may be making tomorrow, either for your own child or someone else's.

Enjoy the twenty-four projects in the following pages; let them express your love and cuddle the love of your life. Whether you're making an heirloom or a basic blankie—just pick a pattern, grab some yarn, and get ready to **KNIT ON THE GO!**

THE BASICS

What is more heartfelt than making a baby blanket that will be passed on from generation to generation? Whether a brightly colored throw, a spread with a whimsical motif, or a sweet crib cover, this book is filled with blankets that will be treasured for years to come, even if they don't take years to knit. Many of the designs are quick and easy, making them stress free if you're crunched for time or need a last-minute gift. Some feature squares or strips that are later assembled during finishing for a truly "on-the-go" project, while others require little more than casting on and binding off. Whatever your taste or skill, there is sure to be a blanket in this collection that will inspire interest and excitement.

All the designs in this book can be altered in size to make them larger or smaller. To adjust most patterns, you can use the traditional method of increasing or decreasing the number of stitches and rows, as well as add or subtract squares, to achieve the desired size. You can also change the yarn weight and/or needle size to create a custom-sized blanket. Remember to adjust yarn requirements and the number of stitches around the edge accordingly.

FINISHING

Since blankets are frequently knit in one piece, keep finishing in mind when beginning your blanket project.

1. Because the back-side of the fabric will be seen when the blanket is used, you must be ready for the reverse to be on display. Think about using a stitch that is reversible, or one that looks good on both sides, such at the Eyelet Squares Blanket on page 28.

2. Consider adding border stitches to your blanket so that it has a built-in finish (many border stitches will also help the blanket lie flat).

3. When adding a new yarn, be careful to do so at a place where you can easily weave the ends in, such as the sides, as there is frequently no "wrong side" on a blanket.

4. Consider adding a fabric backing as a whimsical and practical accent to your fine handwork.

ASSEMBLY

There are several ways to construct a blanket: all in one piece, in squares, in strips, or in sections. If the blanket is knit in one piece, try working back and forth on a long circular needle (29"–60"/74cm –150cm). It will make it easier to accommodate the large number of stitches and keep you from poking the person next to you with your needle if you're working on a bus, train or plane. An edging may be necessary to make the blanket lie flat—in some designs the border is knit in, in others it is picked up and knit or crocheted after the blanket is completed.

GAUGE

Most blanket patterns don't rely on perfect fit as a garment would, but it is still important to knit a gauge swatch. If the gauge is incorrect, a colorwork pattern may become distorted. The type of needles used—straight or circular, wood or metal—will influence gauge, so knit your swatch with the needles you plan to use for the project. Measure gauge as illustrated here. (Launder and block your gauge swatch before taking measurements). Try different needle sizes until your sample measures the required number of stitches and rows. To get fewer stitches to the inch/cm, use larger needles; to get more stitches to the inch/cm, use smaller needles. It's a good idea to keep your gauge swatch to test any embroidery or embellishemnt, and blocking and cleaning methods.

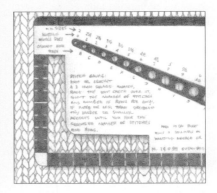

A pieced blanket is particularly suited to knitting on the run or sharing the work with others for a group gift. In this method, the pieces that make up the blanket are knit separately, then joined together to form the finished piece. Try using a contrasting color to join the pieces together and make this a feature of your design.

Joining can be done using these methods:

1. Sewing, using the traditional seaming method used for sweaters.

2. Crocheting, using either slip stitch or single crochet.

3. Embroidery, using a decorative stitch such as whip stitch or herringbone.

BLOCKING

Blocking is the best way to shape pattern pieces and smooth knitted edges. However, some yarns, such as chenilles and ribbons, do not benefit from blocking. Choose a blocking method using information on the yarn care label and, when in doubt, test-block your gauge swatch.

Wet Block Method

Using rust-proof pins, pin the finished blanket to measurements on a flat surface and lightly dampen using a spray bottle. Allow to dry before removing the pins.

Steam Block Method

Pin the finished blanket to measurements with the wrong side of the knitting facing up. Steam lightly, holding the iron 2"/5cm above the work. Do not press the iron onto the knitting as it will flatten the stitches.

BACKING

Adding a fabric backing to your blanket has several advantages. It hides the sometimes unfinished look of the "wrong side" of the knitting, adds warmth, and can add an interesting design element. The best fabrics to use are flannel, brushed cotton, cotton knit, or polar fleece, as these fabrics wash well and are soft to the touch. Before sewing on the backing, preshrink the fabric. Fold the fabric edges under 1"/2.5cm on all sides and press in place. (If using fleece, skip this step and simply cut the fabric to the size of the blanket.) With wrong sides together, pin the backing to the blanket and slip stitch together on all sides. Tack the backing to the blanket at random intervals to prevent bagging.

YARN SELECTION

For an exact reproduction of the blanket photographed, use the yarn listed in the materials section of the pattern. We've selected yarns that are readily available in the U.S. and Canada at the time of printing. The Resources list on page 94 provides addresses of yarn distributors. Contact them for the name of a retailer in your area.

YARN SUBSTITUTION

You may wish to substitute yarns. Perhaps a spectacular yarn matches your baby's bedroom, maybe you view small-scale projects as a chance to incorporate leftovers from your yarn stash, or the yarn specified may not be available in your area. Blankets allow you to be creative, but you'll need to knit to the given gauge to obtain the knitted measurements with the substitute yarn (see "Gauge" on page 11). Make pattern adjustments where necessary. Be sure to consider how different yarn types (chenille, mohair, bouclé, etc.) will affect the final appearance of your blanket, and how it will feel against the baby's skin.

Some of the most common fibers used for babies are acrylic baby yarns, which are soft, lightweight and machine-washable; baby wools, which have incredible warmth; and cottons which are most suitable for warmer climates.

To facilitate yarn substitution, Vogue Knitting grades yarn by the standard stitch gauge obtained in stockinette stitch. You'll find a grading number in the "Materials" section of the pattern, immediately following the yarn. Look for a substitute yarn that falls into the same category. The suggested needle size and gauge on the ball band should be comparable to that on the Standard Yarn Weight chart on page 13.

After you've successfully gauge-swatched a substitute yarn, you'll need to figure out how much of the substitute yarn the project requires. First, find the total length of the original yarn in the pattern (multiply number of balls by yards/meters per ball). Divide this figure by the new yards/meters per ball (listed on the ball band). Round up to the next whole number. The answer is the number of balls required.

Categories of yarn, gauge ranges and recommended needle and hook sizes

Yarn Weight Symbol & Category Names	Super Fine	Fine	Light	Medium	Bulky	Super Bulky
Type of Yarns in Category	Sock, Fingering, Baby	Sport, Baby	DK, Light Worsted	Worsted, Afghan, Aran	Chunky, Craft, Rug	Super Bulky Roving
Knit Gauge Range* in Stockinette Stitch to 4 inches	27–32 sts	23–26 sts	21–24 sts	16–20 sts	12–15 sts	6–11 sts
Recommended Needle in Metric Size Range	2.25–3.25 mm	3.25–3.75 mm	3.75–4.5 mm	4.5–5.5 mm	5.5–8 mm	9–15 mm and larger
Recommended Needle U.S. size range	1 to 3	3 to 5	5 to 7	7 to 9	9 to 11	11 to 19 and larger
Crochet Gauge* Ranges in Single Crochet to 4 inch	21–32 sts	16–20 sts	12–17 sts	11–14 sts	8–11 sts	5–9 sts
Recommended Hook in Metric Size Range	2.25–3.5 mm	3.5–4.5 mm	4.5–5.5 mm	5.5–6.5 mm	6.5–9 mm	9–12 mm and larger
Recommended Hook U.S. Size Range	B-1 to E-4	E-4 to 7	7 to I-9	I-9 to K-10½	K-10½ to M-13	M-13 to P-16 and larger

Beginner

Ideal first project.

Intermediate

For knitters with some experience. More intricate stitches, shaping and finishing.

Very Easy Very Vogue

Basic stitches, minimal shaping, simple finishing.

Experienced

For knitters able to work patterns with complicated shaping and finishing.

CROCHET STITCHES

CHAIN

1 *Pass the yarn over the hook and catch it with the hook.*

2 *Draw the yarn through the loop on the hook.*

3 *Repeat steps 1 and 2 to make a chain.*

SINGLE CROCHET

1 *Insert the hook through top two loops of a stitch. Pass the yarn over the hook and draw up a loop—two loops on hook.*

2 *Pass the yarn over the hook and draw through both loops on hook.*

3 *Continue in the same way, inserting the hook into each stitch.*

HALF-DOUBLE CROCHET

1 *Pass the yarn over the hook. Insert the hook through the top two loops of a stitch.*

2 *Pass the yarn over the hook and draw up a loop—three loops on hook. Pass the yarn over the hook.*

3 *Draw through all three loops on hook.*

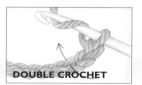

DOUBLE CROCHET

1 *Pass the yarn over the hook. Insert the hook through the top two loops of a stitch.*

2 *Pass the yarn over the hook and draw up a loop— three loops on hook.*

3 *Pass the yarn over the hook and draw it through the first two loops on the hook, pass the yarn over the hook and draw through the remaining two loops. Continue in the same way, inserting the hook into each stitch.*

SLIP STITCH

Insert the crochet hook into a stitch, catch the yarn and pull up a loop. Draw the loop through the loop on the hook.

Illustrations: Joni Coniglio

FOLLOWING CHARTS

Charts provide a convenient way to follow colorwork, lace, cable and other stitch patterns at a glance. Vogue Knitting stitch charts utilize the universal knitting language of "symbolcraft." Unless otherwise indicated, read charts from right to left on right side (RS) rows and from left to right on wrong side (WS) rows, repeating any stitch and row repeats as directed in the pattern. Posting a self-adhesive note under your working row is an easy way to keep track of your place on a chart.

COLORWORK KNITTING

Two main types of colorwork are explored in this book.

Intarsia

Intarsia is accomplished with separate bobbins of individual colors. This method is ideal for large blocks of color or for motifs that aren't repeated close together, such as the Sheep Motif Blanket on page 18. When changing colors, always pick up the new color and wrap around the old color to prevent holes.

Stranding

When motifs are closely placed, colorwork is accomplished by stranding along two or more colors per row, creating "floats" on the wrong side of the fabric. When using this method, twist yarns on WS to prevent holes and strand loosely to keep knitting from puckering.

Note that yarn amounts have been calculated for the colorwork method suggested in the pattern. Knitting a stranded pattern with intarsia bobbins will take less yarn, while stranding an intarsia pattern will require more yarn.

CARE

Refer to the yarn label for the recommended cleaning method. Many of the blankets in the book can be either washed by hand, or in the machine on a gentle or wool cycle, in lukewarm water with a mild detergent. Do not agitate, and don't soak for more than 10 minutes. Rinse gently with tepid water, then fold in a towel and gently press the water out. Lay flat to dry away from excess heat and light. Check the yarn band for any specific care instructions such as dry cleaning or tumble drying.

TASSELS

Cut a piece of cardboard to the desired length of the tassel. Wrap yarn around the cardboard. Knot a piece of yarn tightly around one end, cut as shown, and remove the cardboard. Wrap and tie yarn around the tassel about 1"/2.5cm down from the top to secure the fringe.

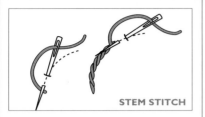

STEM STITCH

SATIN STITCH

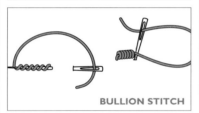

BULLION STITCH

CHAIN STITCH

FRENCH KNOT

WORKING A YARN OVER

Between two knit stitches: Bring the yarn from the back of the work to the front between the two needles. Knit the next stitch, bringing the yarn to the back over the right-hand needle, as shown.

STANDARD BLANKET SIZES

Use these measurements as a guide– you may need to adjust them to accommodate stitch and color patterns and repeats.

■ **Receiving**

30"-36"/76cm-91.5cm square

■ **Carriage**

24"-30"/61cm-76cm square

18"-24"/45.5cm-61cm wide x 24"-30"/61cm-76cm long

■ **Crib**

36"-42"/91.5-106.5cm square

34"-40"/86cm-101.5cm wide x 38"-44"/96.5cm-111.5cm long.

■ **Throw/Afghan**

34"-44"/101.5cm-111.5cm wide x 38"-48"/96.5cm-122cm long.

KNITTING TERMS AND ABBREVIATIONS

approx approximately

beg begin(ning)

bind off Used to finish an edge and keep stitches from unraveling. Lift the first stitch over the second, the second over the third, etc. (UK: cast off)

cast on A foundation row of stitches placed on the needle in order to begin knitting.

CC contrast color

ch chain(s)

cm centimeter(s)

cn cable needle

cont continu(e)(ing)

dc double crochet (UK: treble)

dec decrease(ing)—Reduce the stitches in a row (knit 2 together).

dpn double pointed needle(s)

foll follow(s)(ing)

g gram(s)

garter stitch Knit every row. Circular knitting: knit one round, then purl one round.

hdc half-double crochet (UK: htr-half treble)

inc increase(ing)—Add stitches in a row (knit into the front and back of a stitch).

k knit

k2tog knit 2 stitches together

lp(s) loops(s)

LH left-hand

m meter(s)

M1 make one stitch—With the needle tip, lift the strand between last stitch worked and next stitch on the left-hand needle and knit into the back of it. One stitch has been added.

MC main color

mm millimeter(s)

oz ounce(s)

p purl

p2tog purl 2 stitches together

pat pattern

pick up and knit (purl) Knit (or purl) into the loops along an edge.

pm place marker—Place or attach a loop of contrast yarn or purchased stitch marker as indicated.

rem remain(s)(ing)

rep repeat

rev St st reverse Stockinette stitch—Purl right-side rows, knit wrong-side rows. Circular knitting: purl all rounds. (UK: reverse stocking stitch)

rnd(s) round(s)

RH right-hand

RS right side(s)

sc single crochet (UK: dc - double crochet)

sk skip

SKP Slip 1, knit 1, pass slip stitch over knit 1.

SK2P Slip 1, knit 2 together, pass slip stitch over k2tog.

sl slip—An unworked stitch made by passing a stitch from the left-hand to the right-hand needle as if to purl.

sl st slip stitch (UK: single crochet)

ssk slip, slip, knit—Slip next 2 stitches knitwise, one at a time, to right-hand needle. Insert tip of left-hand needle into fronts of these stitches from left to right. Knit them together. One stitch has been decreased.

st(s) stitch(es)

St st Stockinette stitch—Knit right-side rows, purl wrong-side rows. Circular knitting: knit all rounds. (UK: stocking stitch)

tbl through back of loop

tog together

tr treble crochet (UK: dtr-double treble)

WS wrong side(s)

w&t wrap and turn

wyif with yarn in front

wyib with yarn in back

work even Continue in pattern without increasing or decreasing. (UK: work straight)

yd yard(s)

yo yarn over—Make a new stitch by wrapping the yarn over the right-hand needle (UK: yfwd, yon, yrn)

* Repeat directions following * as many times as indicated.

[ ] Repeat directions inside brackets as many times as indicated.

SHEEP MOTIF BLANKET

Baa, baa black sheep...

■■■▢

This sweet pastoral scene lends rustic charm to a farm-friendly throw. The sheep come to life in textured novelty yarn; patches of grass are embroidered in the finishing. Designed by Jean Guirguis.

KNITTED MEASUREMENTS
■ Approx 27" x 31"/68.5cm x 78.5cm

MATERIALS
■ 9 1¾oz/50g balls (each approx 55yd/ 50m) of Berroco, Inc. *Pronto* (cotton/ acrylic) in #4430 green (A) (5)
■ 1 1¾ oz/50g balls (each approx 90yd/ 83m) of Berroco, Inc. *Plush* (nylon) each in #1901 white (B) and #1934 black (C) (6)
■ One pair size 9 (5.5mm) needles *or size to obtain gauge*

GAUGE
14 sts and 22 rows to 4"/10cm over St st using size 9 (5.5mm) needles and *Pronto*. *Take time to check gauge.*

Note
When changing colors, twist yarns on WS to prevent holes in work. Use a separate bobbin of yarn for each large block of color. When working sheep motifs, use 2 strands of B or C held tog for dense fabric.

SEED STITCH
Row 1 (RS) *K1, p1; rep from * to end.
Row 2 K the purl sts and p the knits sts.
Rep row 2 for seed st.

BLANKET
With A, cast on 96 sts.
Work 10 rows in seed st.
Beg chart pat
Next row (RS) Work 7 sts seed st, row 1 of chart over next 82 sts, 7 sts seed st. Cont in pats as established through row 150 of chart pat.
With A, work 10 rows in seed st. Bind off in pat.

FINISHING
Block blanket lightly to measurements.
Embroidery
With A, using long and short stem stitches, embroider grass clumps as indicated on chart.

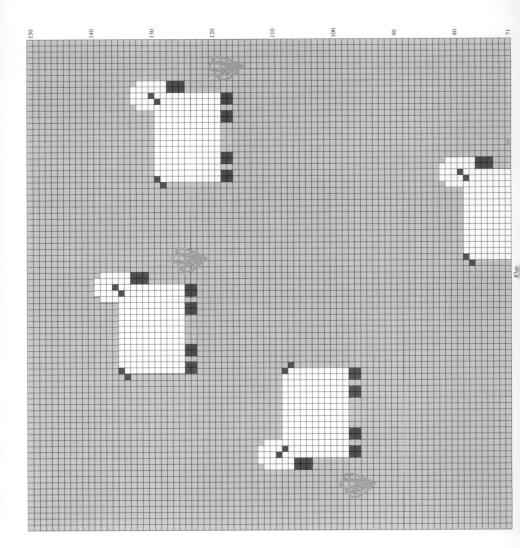

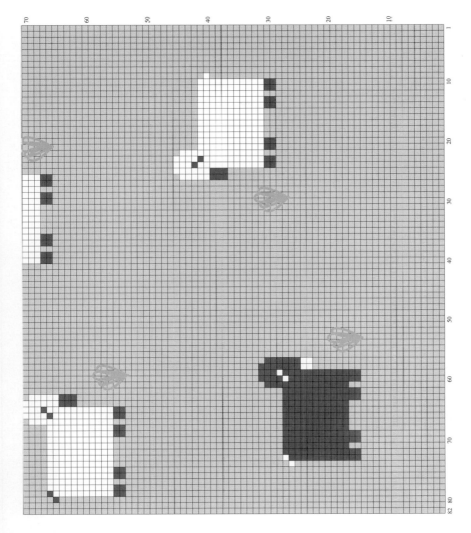

Color Key

- ▢ Green (A)
- ☐ White (B)
- ■ Black (C)

CABLED AND RIBBED COVERLET

Do the twist

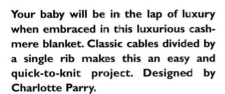

Your baby will be in the lap of luxury when embraced in this luxurious cashmere blanket. Classic cables divided by a single rib makes this an easy and quick-to-knit project. Designed by Charlotte Parry.

KNITTED MEASUREMENTS
■ Approx 30" x 30"/76cm x 76cm

MATERIALS
■ 5 3½oz/100g (each approx 165yd/140m) of Trendsetter Yarns *Dali* (cashmere) in #192 camel (5)
■ One size 9 (5.5mm) circular needle 29"/74cm long *or size to obtain gauge*
■ *Cable needle (cn)*

GAUGE
25 sts and 24 rows to 4"/10cm over cable pat using size 9 (5.5mm) needles.
Take time to check gauge.

STITCH GLOSSARY
6-st RC
Sl 3 sts to cn and hold to back, k3, k3 from cn.

BLANKET
Cast on 161 sts. Work in garter st for 6 rows, inc 15 sts evenly across last row— 176 sts.

Row 1 (RS) K6, *p2, k6, p2, k1; rep from * to last 5 sts, k5.

Row 2 and all WS rows K5, *p1, k2, p6, k2; rep from * to last 6 sts, p1, k5.

Row 3 K6, *p2, 6-st RC, p2, k1; rep from * to last 5 sts, k5.

Rows 5 and 7 Rep row 1.

Row 8 Rep row 2.

Rep rows 1-8 for cable pat until blanket measures approx 29"/74cm ending with row 4 of pat.

Next row (RS) K, dec 15 sts evenly— 161 sts.

Work 5 rows in garter st. Bind off.

FINISHING
Block to measurements.

FELTED BLANKET
Fulling around

Easy as 1-2-3, this cozy throw is loosely worked in stockinette and accentuated with seed-stitch edges. The entire blanket is then felted for the warmest blanket baby owns. Designed by Gretchen Strahle.

KNITTED MEASUREMENTS
■ Approx 37" x 43"/94cm x 109cm (before felting)
■ Approx 27" x 32"/68.5cm x 81.5cm (after felting)

MATERIALS
■ 5 1¾oz/50g skeins (each approx 108yd/100m) Noro/KFI *Kureyon* (wool) each in #102 (A) and #95 (B)
■ One size 6 (4mm) circular needle 36"/90cm long *or size to obtain gauge*

GAUGE
14 sts to 4"/10cm over St st using size 6 (4mm) needle (before felting).
Take time to check gauge.

SEED STITCH
Row 1 (RS) *K1, p1; rep from * to end.
Row 2 *P1, k1; rep from * to end.
Rep last 2 rows for seed st.

STRIPE PAT
Row 1 (RS) With B, work 6 sts in seed st, k to last 6 sts, work 6 sts in seed st.
Row 2 Work 6 sts in seed st, p to last 6 sts, work 6 sts in seed st.
Rows 3 and 4 Rep last 2 rows once.
Rows 5 to 8 With A, rep last 4 rows once.
Rep last 8 rows for stripe pat.

Note Carry yarn up side of work when working stripes.

BLANKET
With A, cast on 130 sts.
Working back and forth in rows, work 6 rows in seed st.
Work in stripe pat until piece measures approx 42"/106.5cm from beg, end with 8th row of stripe pat.
With B, work 6 rows in seed st. Bind off.

FINISHING
Felting
Weave in all yarn ends Set your washing machine at lowest water level (enough to just cover blanket), hottest temperature and highest agitation. Add blanket and small amount of liquid detergent. Begin washing and check on blanket approx every 5 minutes until desired felting of fabric is achieved; the stitch definition should be almost unrecognizable. Remove blanket and rinse by hand in lukewarm water. Roll blanket in towels to remove excess water. Dry flat.

TEXTURED BLANKET
Cable comfort

■■■▢

Gentle cables are twisted on both sides of this soft, reversible throw; while seed stitch divides the vertical textures. Designed by Norah Gaughan.

KNITTED MEASUREMENTS
■ Approx 32" x 32"/81.5 x 81.5cm

MATERIALS
■ 16 .88oz/25g balls (each approx 76yd/70m) of Artful Yarns/JCA *Virtue* (cashmere) in #5 fortitude ▨
■ Size 7 (4.5mm) circular needle 29"/74cm long *or size to obtain gauge*
■ Cable needle (cn)

GAUGE
26 sts and 28 rows to 4"/10cm over cable pat using size 7 (4.5mm) needles.
Take time to check gauge.

STITCH GLOSSARY
Right twist (RT) Pass in front of first st and k 2nd st, then k first st and let both sts fall from needle.
6-st RPC Sl next 3 sts to cn and hold to *back*, k1, p1, k1, then from cn work k1, p1, k1.

CABLE PATTERN
Row 1 (RS) [K1, p1, k1, p2, k1, p1, RT, p1, k1, p2] 16 times, k1, p1, k1.
Row 2 and all WS rows [K1, p1 k1, RT, p1, k1, p2, k1, p1, RT] 16 times, k1, p1, k1.
Row 3 [K1, p1, k1, p2, 6-st RPC, p2, k1, p1, k1, p2, k1, p1, RT, p1, k1, p2] 8 times, k1, p1, k1.
Rows 5 and 7 Rep row 1.
Row 9 [K1, p1, k1, p2, k1, p1, RT, p1, k1, p2, k1, p1, k1, p2, 6-st RPC, p2] 8 times, k1, p1, k1.
Row 11 Rep row 1.
Row 12 Rep row 2.
Rep rows 1-12 for cable pat.

BLANKET
Cast on 211 sts. Work in cable pat until piece measures 32"/81.5cm, end with a WS row. Bind off.

FINISHING
Lightly block blanket to measurements.

Pretty tumbling blocks of lace and reverse stockinette are worked on the bias in this airy blanket. A cashmere/cotton blend yarn keeps baby soft and warm. Designed by Linda Cyr.

KNITTED MEASUREMENTS
■ Approx 32" x 32"/81.5cm x 81.5cm

MATERIALS
■ 6 1¾oz/50g (each approx 125yd/114m) of Classic Elite Yarn *Inspiration* (cashmere/cotton) in #93057 pink

■ One size 6 (4mm) circular needle 29"/74cm long *or size to obtain gauge*

GAUGE
22 sts and 30 rows to 4"/10cm over St st using size 6 (4mm) needles.
Take time to check gauge.

Note
For selvages, slip first st of every row purlwise with yarn in front, then take yarn to back between needles, k last st of every row.

STITCH GLOSSARY
Eyelet Panel
(worked across 9 sts)
Rows 1-4 Knit.
Row 5 (WS) K2, [k2tog, yo] twice, k3.
Rows 6-8 Knit.
Row 9 K1, [k2tog, yo] 3 times, k2.
Rows 10-12 Knit.
Rows 13-16 Rep rows 5-8.

Rep rows 1 - 16 for eyelet panel.

BLANKET
Cast on 11 sts. Keeping first and last sts as selvage, work 16 rows of eyelet panel over center 9 sts.

Next row (WS) Cast on 9 sts and work as foll: 1 selvage st, row 1 of eyelet panel over next 9 sts, k9 (for rev St st block), 1 selvage st—20 sts.

Next row Cast on 9 sts and work as foll: 1 selvage st, row 2 of eyelet panel over next 9 sts, p9, row 2 of eyelet panel over next 9 sts, 1 selvage st—29 sts.

Work 14 more rows in pat and rev St st, ending on row 16 of eyelet panel.

Next row Cast on 9 sts and work as foll: 1 selvage st, [k9 (for rev St st block), row 1 of eyelet panel over next 9 sts] twice, 1 selvage st—38 sts.

Next row Cast on 9 sts and work as foll: 1 selvage st, [p9, row 2 of eyelet panel over next 9 sts] twice, p9, 1 selvage st—47 sts.

Work 14 more rows in pat and rev St st, ending on row 16 of eyelet panel.

Cont to add panel blocks every 16 rows in this way, alternating rev St st and eyelet panel blocks, until center section is 23 blocks wide (209 sts), complete panels and end with a WS row.

*Bind off 9 sts at beg of next 2 rows, work 14 more rows to complete eyelet panels. Rep from * until final eyelet block is complete. Bind off rem 11 sts.

FINISHING
Block lightly to measurements.

FLORAL SQUARES COVERLET

A pocket full of posies

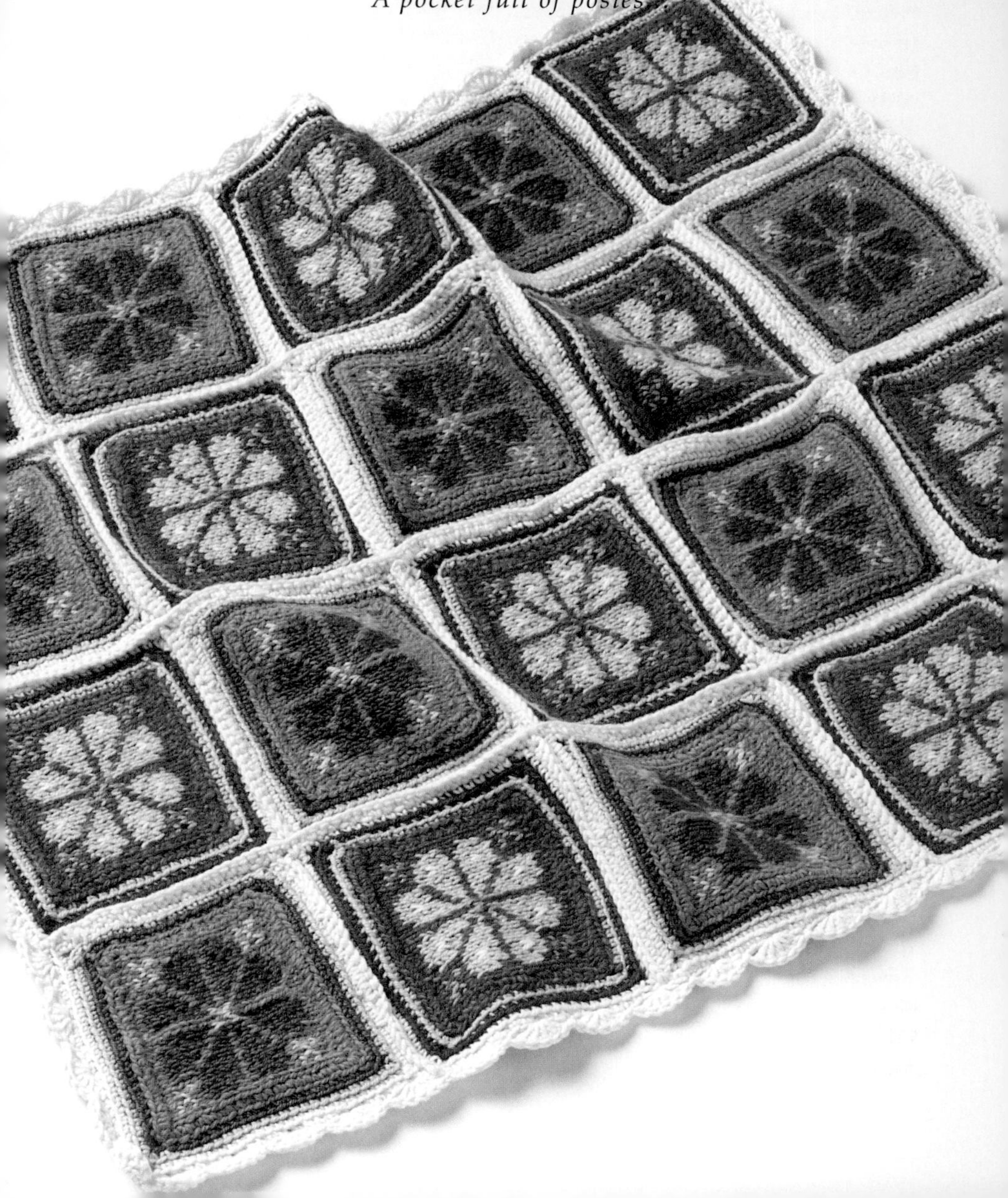

■ ■ ■ ▢

Pretty squares of Fair Isle flowers are knit separately then outlined with crochet stripes. A crochet shell stitch creates the charming edging. Designed by Sasha Kagan.

KNITTED MEASUREMENTS
■ Approx 22" x 26"/56cm x 66cm

MATERIALS
■ 2 1¾oz/50g balls (each approx 123yd/113m) of Rowan Yarns *Wool/Cotton* (wool/cotton) in #900 ecru (A) **③**
■ 1 ball each in #951 lt pink (C), #949 aqua (D), #953 blue (F), #941 lt blue (G) and #943 dk rose (H)
■ 1 1¾oz/50g balls (each approx 123yd/113m) of Rowan Yarns *Yorkshire Tweed DK* (wool) each in #350 rose (B) and #349 green (E) **③**
■ One pair size 5 (3.75mm) needles or *size to obtain gauge*
■ Size B/1 (2.25mm) crochet hook

GAUGE
23 sts and 27 rows to 4"/10cm over Fair Isle pat with size 5 (3.75mm) needles.
Take time to check gauge.

Note
Carry yarn not in use loosely across back of work.

BLANKET
Fair Isle squares (make 10 each from charts A and B)

With background shade (B or E), cast on 23 sts.
Work in chart pat through row 23. Bind off.

CROCHET EDGING (CHART A SQUARES)
Rnd 1 With RS of work facing and crochet hook, join B with sl st to any corner of square. Ch 1, work sc evenly around, working 3 sc in corners; join with C sl st to first sc.
Rnd 2 With C, ch 1, working in back loops only of each st, work sc evenly around, working 3 sc in corners; join H with sl st to first sc.
Rnd 3 With H, rep rnd 2.
Rnd 4 With A, rep rnd 2. Fasten off.

CROCHET EDGING (CHART B SQUARES)
Work as for crochet edging of chart A squares using E, F, G and A.

FINISHING
Join Squares
Join squares into 4 strips, 5 squares long alternating square A with square B as shown. Place WS of squares tog, and with A, work 1 row of sc through both thicknesses to join tops and bottoms of squares to form strips 5 squares long. Join 4 strips tog in same way.

CROCHET BORDER
Rnd 1 With RS facing and crochet hook, join A with sl st to bottom right corner of blanket, *work 117 sc to next corner, 3 sc in corner, 102 sc to next corner, 3 sc in

corner; rep from * once more; join with sl st to first sc—450 sc.

Rnd 2 Ch 1, sc in first sc, *sk next 2 sc, 5 dc in next sc, sk next 2 sc, sc in next sc; rep from * around; join with sl st to first sc. Fasten off.

Block blanket to measurements.

Chart A

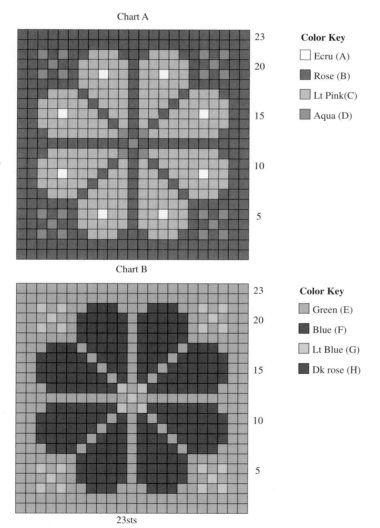

23
20
15
10
5

Color Key

☐ Ecru (A)
■ Rose (B)
☐ Lt Pink(C)
■ Aqua (D)

Chart B

23
20
15
10
5

Color Key

☐ Green (E)
■ Blue (F)
☐ Lt Blue (G)
■ Dk rose (H)

23sts

VINTAGE BLANKET

Little boy blue

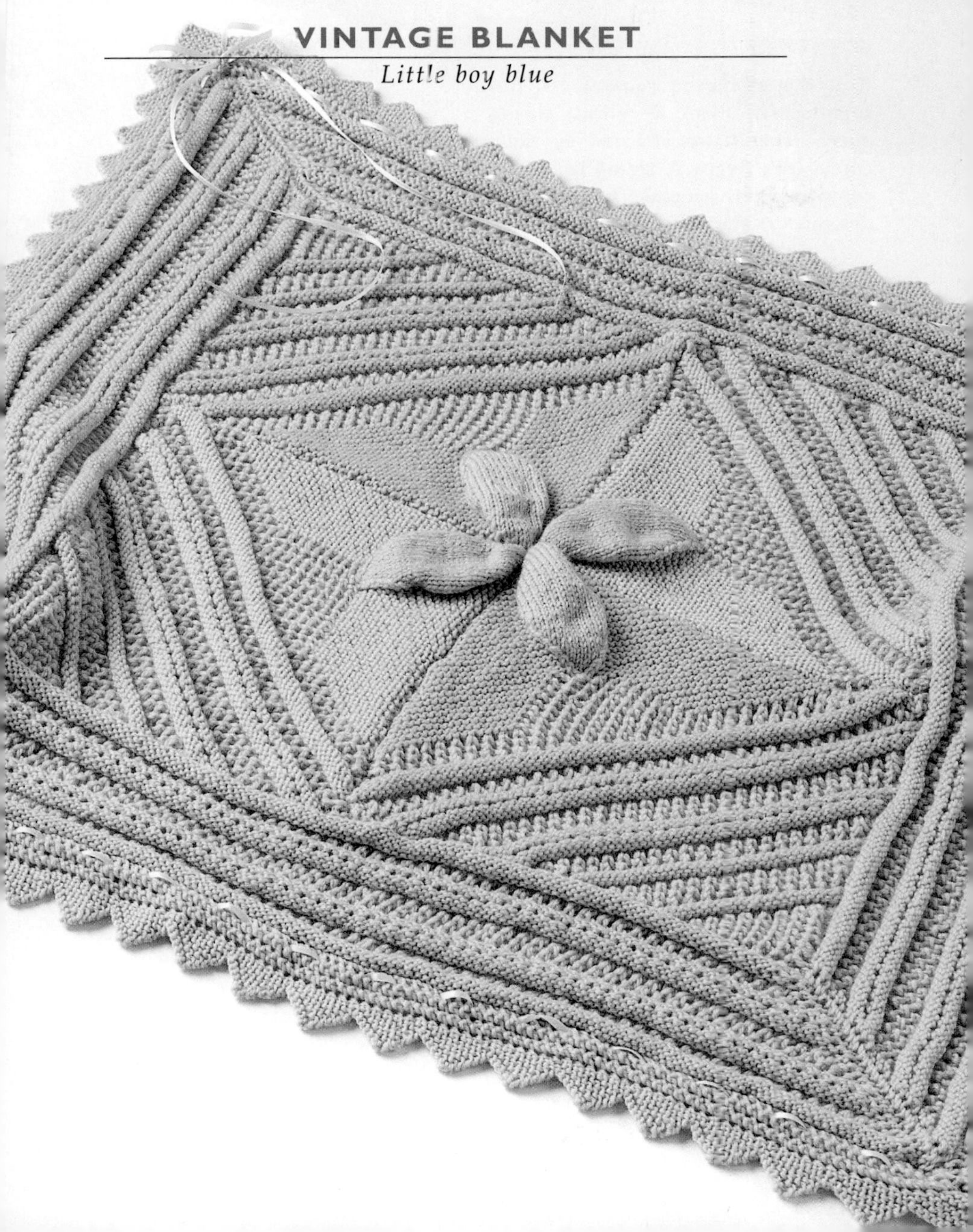

■■■▶

Exquisite embossed squares are put together to form a central three-dimensional flower framed by deep corrugated ridges. A zigzag lace edge completes this keepsake baby blanket designed by Mari Lynn Patrick.

KNITTED MEASUREMENTS
■ Approx 26"/66cm square

MATERIALS
■ 6 1¾ oz/50g balls (each approx 195yd/180m) of Anny Blatt *Baby Blatt* (wool) in #358 lt blue (■2■)
■ One pair size 2 (2.5mm) needles or *size to obtain gauge*
■ Size B/1 (2mm) crochet hook
■ 4yd/3.7m of ⅛-inch/3mm ecru ribbon

GAUGE
One quarter square is 8 ½"/21.5cm square
28 sts and 56 rows to 4"/10cm over garter st using size 2 (2.5mm) needles.
Take time to check gauge.

Note
This blanket is constructed by working 4 quarter squares from the center point outwards and then joining these 4 squares to form one large central square. Each edge of the 4 squares is picked up and worked outwards, then a lengthwise knit trim is worked in four strips to trim the four sides. This same concept could be multiplied outwards to make a bedspread simply by working more central squares to the size desired.

STITCH GLOSSARY
LRD K2tog by inserting needle through front loops first of 2nd st then first and k2tog from this position.
RLD Sl 2 sts, one at a time knitwise, return to LH needle, and k2tog from this position.

QUARTER SQUARE
(make 4)
Cast on 1 st.
Row 1 Yo, k1.
Row 2 Yo, k2.
Row 3 [Yo, k1] 3 times.
Row 4 Yo, k1, p3, k2.
Row 5 Yo, k2, yo, k3, yo, k2.
Row 6 Yo, k2, p5, k3.
Row 7 Yo, k3, yo, k5, yo, k3.
Row 8 Yo, k3, p7, k4.
Row 9 Yo, k4, yo, k7, yo, k4.
Row 10 Yo, k4, p9, k5.
Row 11 Yo, k5, yo, k9, yo, k5.
Row 12 Yo, k5, p11, k6.
Row 13 Yo, k6, yo, k11, yo, k6.
Row 14 Yo, k6, p13, k7.
Row 15 Yo, k7, yo, k13, yo, k7.
Row 16 Yo, k7, p15, k8.
Row 17 Yo, k31.
Row 18 Yo, k8, p15, k9
Row 19 and all odd rows through row 29 Yo, k rem sts.
Row 20 Yo, k9, p15, k10.
Row 22 Yo, k10, p15, k11.
Row 24 Yo, k11, p15, k12.
Row 26 Yo, k12, p15, k13.
Row 28 Yo, k13, p15, k14.
Row 30 Yo, k14, p15, k15.
Row 31 Yo, k15, RLD, k28.

Row 32 Yo, k15, p2tog, p12, k16.
Row 33 Yo, k16, RLD, k27.
Row 34 Yo, k16, p2tog, p10, k17.
Row 35 Yo, k17, RLD, k26.
Row 36 Yo, k17, p2tog, p8, k18.
Row 37 Yo, k18, RLD, k25.
Row 38 Yo, k18, p2tog, p6, k19.
Row 39 Yo, k19, RLD, k24.
Row 40 Yo, k19, p2tog, p4, k20.
Row 41 Yo, k20, RLD, k23.
Row 42 Yo, k20, p2tog, p2, k21.
Row 43 Yo, k21, RLD, k22.
Row 44 Yo, k21, [yo, LRD] twice, k20.
Row 45 Yo, k46.
Row 46 Yo, k21, [yo, LRD] 3 times, k20.
Row 47 and all odd-numbered rows through row 67 Yo, k rem sts.
Row 48 Yo, k21, [yo, LRD] 4 times, k20.
Row 50 Yo, k21, [yo, LRD] 5 times, k20.
Row 52 and all even-numbered rows through row 60 Yo, k21, [yo, LRD] once more than the previous even-numbered rows, k20. On row 60, the repeat after brackets will be worked 10 times.
Row 62 Yo, k1, [yo, LRD] 31 times.
Row 64 Yo, k1, [yo, LRD] 32 times.
Row 66 Yo, k1, [yo, LRD] 33 times.
Row 68 Yo, p69.
Row 69 Yo, k70.
Row 70 Yo, k71.
Row 71 Yo, p72.
Row 72 Yo, k73.
Row 73 Yo, p74.
Row 74 Yo, k75.
Row 75 Yo, k76.
Row 76 Yo, p77.
Row 77 Yo, k78.

Row 78 Yo, k1, [yo, LRD] 39 times.
Row 79 RLD, k78.
Row 80 RLD, [yo, LRD] 38 times, k1.
Row 81 RLD, k76.
Row 82 P2tog, p75.
Row 83 RLD, k74.
Row 84 RLD, k73.
Row 85 P2tog, p72.
Row 86 RLD, k71.
Row 87 RLD, [yo, LRD] 35 times.
Row 88 RLD, k69.
Row 89 P2tog, p68.
Row 90 RLD, k67
Row 91 RLD, k66.
Row 92 P2tog, p65.
Row 93 RLD, k64.
Row 94 RLD, [yo, LRD] 31 times, k1.
Row 95 RLD, k62.
Row 96 RLD, [yo, LRD] 30 times, k1.
Row 97 RLD, k60.
Row 98 RLD, [yo, LRD] 29 times, k1.
Row 99 RLD, k58.
Row 100 P2tog, p57.
Row 101 RLD, k56.
Row 102 RLD, k55.
Row 103 P2tog, p54.
Row 104 RLD, k53.
Row 105 RLD, [yo, LRD] 26 times.
Row 106 RLD, k51.
Row 107 P2tog, p50.
Row 108 RLD, k49
Row 109 RLD, k48.
Row 110 P2tog, p47.
Row 111 RLD, k46.
Row 112 RLD, [yo, LRD] 22 times, k1.
Row 113 RLD, k44.
Row 114 RLD, [yo, LRD] 21 times, k1.

Row 115 RLD, k42.
Row 116 P2tog, p41.
Row 117 RLD, k40.
Row 118 RLD, k39.
Row 119 P2tog, p38.
Row 120 RLD, k37.
Row 121 RLD, k36.
Row 122 P2tog, p35.
Row 123 RLD, k34.
Row 124 RLD, [yo, LRD] 16 times, k1.
Row 125 RLD, k32.
Row 126 RLD, [yo, LRD] 15 times, k1.
Row 127 RLD, k30.
Row 128 RLD, [yo, LRD] 14 times, k1.
Row 129 RLD, k28.
Row 130 P2tog, p27.
Row 131 RLD, k26.
Row 132 RLD, k25.
Row 133 P2tog, p24.
Row 134 RLD, k23
Row 135 RLD, k22.
Row 136 P2tog, p21.
Row 137 RLD, k20.
Row 138 RLD, [yo, LRD] 9 times, k1.
Row 139 and all odd rows through row 153 RLD, k to end.
Row 140 RLD, [yo, LRD] 8 times, k1.
Row 142 RLD, [yo, LRD] 7 times, k1.
Row 144 and all even rows through row 152 RLD, [yo, LRD] 1 time less than on the previous even-numbered row, k1.
Row 154 RLD, yo, LRD, k1.
Row 155 RLD, k2.
Row 156 Sl the first st, work LRD, then pass the sts just worked tog. Fasten off. Using crochet hook, sl st the 4 quarter squares tog from WS to form central square.

SIDE EDGE

Pick up and k 104 sts along one side edge of central square.
Row 1 (WS) K3, purl to last 3 sts, k3.
Row 2 K2, yo, k to last 2 sts, yo, k2.
Cont to work k3 at beg and end of every WS row and k2, yo at beg and yo, k2 at end of every RS row, AT SAME TIME, work rows 70-120 of quarter square.
Next row (RS) K2, yo, p to last 2 sts, yo, k2.
Next row (WS) Knit.
Next row (RS) K2, yo, k to last 2 sts, yo, k2. Bind off all sts. Work 3 more side edges in same way.

ZIGZAG EDGE

(make 4 strips)
Cast on 9 sts.
Row 1 (RS) K2, [yo, LRD] twice, yo, k3.
Row 2 and all even rows to row 12 Knit.
Row 3 K2, [yo, LRD] twice, yo, k4.
Row 5 K2, [yo, LRD] twice, yo, k5.
Row 7 K2, [yo, LRD] twice, yo, k6.
Row 9 K2, [yo, LRD] twice, yo, k7.
Row 11 K2, [yo, LRD] twice, yo, k8.
Row 12 Bind off 6 sts, k8.
Rep rows 1-12 until there are a total of 20 triangles, end row 12. Work row 1 once more.
Next short row (WS) K4, turn
Next short row (RS) Yo, k4.
Next short row K5, turn.
Next short row Yo, k5.
Next short row K8, turn.
Next short row Yo, LRD, yo, k6.
Next short row K11, turn.

Next short row [Yo, LRD] twice, yo, k7.
Next row K all 14 sts.
Next row Work row 11. Bind off all sts. Pin or baste each edge to the 4 sides of square. With crochet hook from WS, sl st each edge to the sides of square.

Then from RS, sew tog the 4 corners of the square and edges (for a flat seam), curving the short row end of each edging to the beg slanted edge neatly.

Thread the ribbon through the first openwork row of edging.

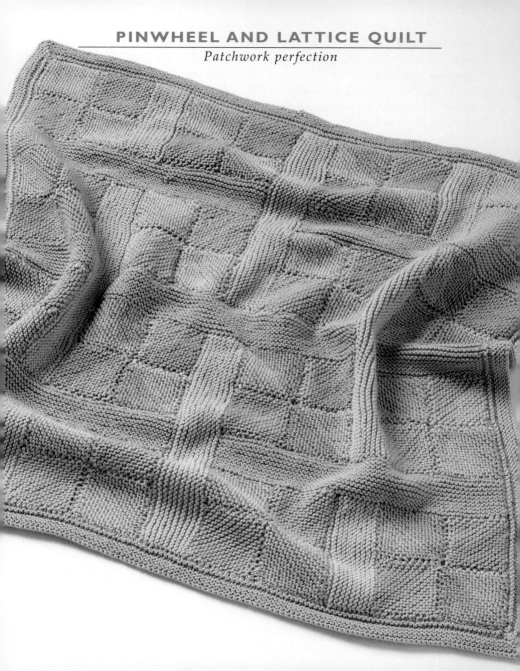

■■■■▶

Garter-stitched squares are sewn together in four quadrants to form a classic quilt pinwheel design; two-toned lattice work links the squares together. Designed by Mari Lynn Patrick.

■ 26½"/67cm x 26½"/67cm square

MATERIALS
■ 4 1¾oz/50g balls (each approx 135yd/125m) of Debbie Bliss/KFI *Baby Cashmerino* (wool/microfiber/cashmere) in #340303 grey (A) **(2)**
■ 2 balls each in #340600 peach (C) and #340202 aqua (D)
■ 1 ball each in #340102 camel (B) and #340608 mauve (E)
■ One pair size 4 (3.5mm) needles *or size to obtain gauge*
■ Size 2 (2.5mm) circular needle, 29"/74cm long

GAUGE
■ 26 sts and 52 rows to 4"/10cm over garter st using size 4 (3.5mm) needles
■ One pinwheel quadrant is 2½"/6.5cm square.
Take time to check gauge.

Notes
1 There is a total of 16 quilt squares, each formed by putting together four matching color quadrants in positions to form a pinwheel design (see layout diagram).
2 The lattice strips, in colors C and D, are worked by picking up sts along the sides of the squares in the numerical order (1-15) and knit in the direction as shown in the layout diagram.

BLANKET
Quadrant
(make 12 in each colorway)
With A, cast on 1 st.
Row 1 K1.
Row 2 (WS) K1 into front, back and front of st.
Row 3 K3.
Row 4 K1 into front and back of first st, k1, k1 into front and back of last st.
Row 5 K5.
Row 6 K1 into front and back of first st, k to last st, k1 into front and back of last st.
Row 7 and all odd rows Knit.
Rows 8, 10, 12, 14, 16, 18 and 20 Rep row 6—21 sts.
Row 21 With A, knit. Cut A. Work rem of quadrant with B, C, D or E.
Row 22 (WS) With B, C, D or E, SKP, k to last 2 sts, k2tog—19 sts.
Row 23 and all odd rows With working contrast color, knit.
Rows 24, 26, 28, 20, 32, 34, 34, 36 and 38 With working contrast color, rep row 22—3 sts.
Last row SK2P. Fasten off.

SQUARE
Foll layout diagram for colors, sew tog 4 quadrants positioned to form the square as shown in layout diagram. Work lattice strips as foll:

Strip 1

With D, pick up and k 30 sts along side of first lower left square as in diagram. K18 rows. Bind off. Join this D pinwheel square to next B pinwheel square by sewing this piece along strip from RS.

Strip 2

With C, pick up and k 30 sts along lower edge of D square and k18 rows in the direction shown. Bind off. Join this D pinwheel square to next E pinwheel square by sewing from RS.

Strip 3

With D, pick up and k 69 sts along the 2 joined side squares and k 18 rows in the direction shown. Bind off.

Strip 4

With C, pick up and k 69 sts along the 2 joined lower squares and k 18 rows in this direction. Bind off.

Strip 5

With D, pick up and k 30 sts along the top square and k 18 rows in the direction shown. Bind off. Sew to side of next top square.

Strip 6

With C, pick up and k 69 sts along the 2 joined squares and k 18 rows in this direction. Bind off.

Strip 7

Sew squares into position, then with D, pick up and k 69 sts along the joined squares and k 18 rows in this direction. Bind off. Cont to work strips in this way, sewing squares tog when necessary, working short strips 8, 10 and 14 with 30 sts in colors as in diagram and strips 9, 11, 12, 13 and 15 with 69 sts in colors as in diagram. Finish by sewing any open ends of squares and strips tog.

FINISHING

Block to measurements.

OUTSIDE EDGE

With C, from RS and circular needle, pick up and k sts along one edge of square as foll: 29 sts along one square, [9 sts along lattice strip, 29 sts along one square] twice —105 sts. Slide sts to opposite end of needle and rejoin C to work first row from RS.

Row 1 (RS) With C, knit.

Row 2 With C, k1 into front and back of first st, (for inc) k to last st, inc 1 st in last st.

Row 3 K1C, *k2D, k2C; rep from * to end.

Row 4 Inc 1C st, *p2C, p2D; rep from *, end inc 1 C st in last st. Cut yarn leaving long ends.

Row 5 (RS) With A, knit.

Row 6 With A, inc 1 st in first st, k to last st, inc 1 st in last st.

Rows 7, 9 and 11 Rep row 5.

Rows 8 and 10 Rep row 6.

Bind off knitwise with A. Using 2 strands C, whip st corners of edging tog as in photo.

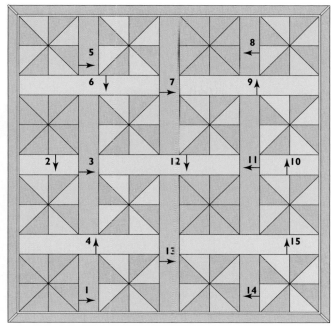

ELEPHANT MOTIF BLANKET

Center ring

■■■▢

Welcome to the jungle! A lush green background provides a lovely setting for intarsia-knit elephants. Their blankets are knitted separately and sewn on later. Crocheted scallops add a pretty finish. Designed by Gitta Schrade.

KNITTED MEASUREMENTS

■ Approx 30" x 30"/76cm x 76cm (excluding crochet edging)

MATERIALS

■ 4 1¾oz/50g balls (each approx 109yd/100m) of Naturally/SR Kertzer *Merino et Soie* (wool/silk) in #105 sage (A) ■■■▢
■ 2 balls each in #104 light blue (B), #100 rose (C), #102 mauve (D), #103 cream (E)
■ Small amounts of black and grey yarn to embroider eyes
■ One pair size 7 (4.5mm) needles *or size to obtain gauge*
■ Size G/6 (4mm) crochet hook for edging

GAUGE

20 sts and 26 rows to 4"/10cm over St st using size 7 (4.5mm) needles.
Take time to check gauge.

Note

When changing colors, twist yarns on WS to prevent holes in work. Use a separate bobbin of yarn for each large block of color.

BLANKET

Center section

With A, cast on 110 sts.
Work in chart pat through row 140. Bind off.

FINISHING

Embroidery

With A, using stem st, embroider elephants' ears as indicated on chart.
With black and grey yarn, using satin st, embroider eyes. With appropriate colors, embroider each elephant's tail using stem st.

LARGE ELEPHANT'S BLANKET

With E, cast on 26 sts.
Row 1 (RS) Purl.
Row 2 Purl.
Row 3 P2 E, k22 D, p2 E.
Row 4 P2 E, p22 D, p2 E.
Row 5 P2 E, k2 A, [k2 C, k2 A] 5 times, p2 E.
Row 6 P2 E, p2 A, [p2 C, p2 A] 5 times, p2 E.
Row 7 P2 E, k2 C, [k2 A, k2 C] 5 times, p2 E.
Row 8 P2 E, p2 C, [p2 A, p2 C] 5 times, p2 E.
Row 9 Rep row 5.
Row 10 Rep row 6.
Row 11 Rep row 3.
Row 12 Rep row 4.
Row 13 P2 E, k22 B, p2 E.
Row 14 P2 E, p22 B, p2 E.
Row 15 P2 E, k22 C, p2 E.
Row 16 P2 E, p22 C, p2 E.
Row 17 P2 E, k2 B, [k2 D, k2 B] 5 times, p2 E.
Row 18 P2 E, p2 B, [p2 D, p2 B] 5 times, p2 E.
Row 19 P2 E, k2 D, [k2 B, k2 D] 5 times, p2 E.

Row 20 P2 E, p2 D, [p2 B, p2 D] 5 times, p2 E.
Row 21 Rep row 17.
Row 22 Rep row 18.
Row 23 P2 E, k22 A, p2 E.
Row 24 P2 E, p22 A, p2 E.
Row 25 P2 E, k22 C, p2 E.
Row 26 P2 E, p22 C, p2 E.
Row 27 Rep row 3.
Row 28 Rep row 4.
Row 29 P2 E, k2 C, [k2 B, k2 C] 5 times, p2 E.
Row 30 P2 E, p2 C, [p2 B, p2 C] 5 times, p2 E.
Row 31 P2 E, k2 B, [k2 C, k2 B] 5 times, p2 E.
Row 32 P2 E, p2 B, [p2 C, p2 B] 5 times, p2 E.
Row 33 Rep row 29.
Row 34 Rep row 30.
Row 35 Rep row 23.
Row 36 P2 E, p22 A, p2tog E.
Row 37 With C, bind off 6 sts, k to last 2 sts, p2 E.
Row 38 P2 E, with C, p to last 2 sts, p2tog.
Row 39 With D, bind off 8 sts, k to last 2 sts, p2 E.
Row 40 P2 E, with D, p to last 2 sts, p2tog.
With D, bind off rem 9 sts.

Sew in position to large elephant between markers indicated on chart.
Make 2 small tassels using colors A, C and D and attach to each bottom corner of blanket.

SMALL ELEPHANT'S BLANKET
With E, cast on 16 sts.
Row 1 (RS) Purl.
Row 2 Purl.
Row 3 P2 E, k12 B, p2 E.
Row 4 P2 E, p12 B, p2 E.
Row 5 P2 E, k12 D, p2 E.
Row 6 P2 E, p12 D, p2 E.
Row 7 P2 E, k12 A, p2 E.
Row 8 P2 E, p12 A, p2 E.
Row 9 P2 E, k12 C, p2 E.
Row 10 P2 E, p12 C, p2 E.
Rows 11 to 18 Rep rows 3 to 10.
Row 19 P2 E, k12 D, p2tog E.
Row 20 With D, bind off 5 sts, p to last 2 sts, p2 E.
Row 21 P2 E, with A, k to last 2 sts, k2tog.
Row 22 With A, bind off 5 sts, p to last 2 sts, p2 E.
Row 23 P2 E, k2tog A.
With E, bind off rem 3 sts.

Sew in position to small elephant between markers indicated on chart.
Make 2 small tassels using colors A, B and D and attach to each bottom corner of blanket.

First border section
With C, cast on 120 sts.
Work 6 rows in garter st.
Work 2 rows in St st.
With B, rep last 8 rows once.
With D, rep last 8 rows once.
With E, rep last 8 rows once.
Bind off.

Second border section

Work as for first border section in stripe sequence B, C, E, D.

Third border section

Work as for first border section in stripe sequence D, E, C, B.

Fourth border section

Work as for first border section in stripe sequence B, D, E, C.

Using photo as a guide, sew border sections in position.

Rnd 1 With RS facing and crochet hook, join A with sl st to bottom right corner of blanket, *work 136 sc to next corner; rep from * 3 times more; join with sl st to first sc—544 sc.

Rnd 2 Ch 4, 6 tr in first sc *skip 3 sc, sc in next sc, skip 3 sc, 7 tr in next sc; rep from * around to last 7 sc; skip 3 sc, sc in next sc, skip last 3 sc; join with sl st to top of ch 4. Fasten off.

Block blanket to measurements.

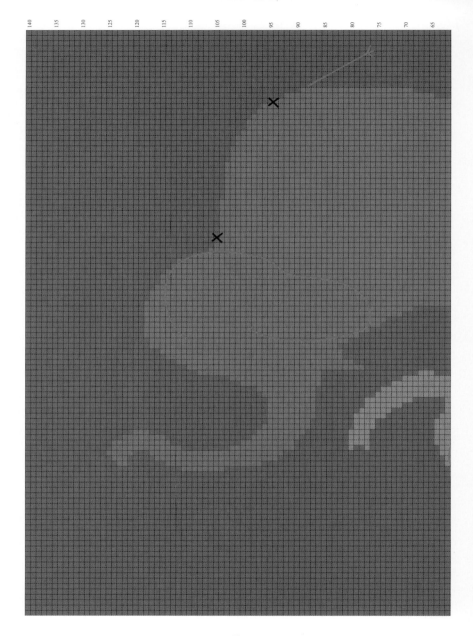

Color Key

Sage (A)

Light Blue (B)

Rose (C)

✗ attach blankets

╱ stem st

110sts

CABLED BLANKET
Sweet dreams

■■■▶

Romantic vintage-style blanket features allover cables and a textured pattern framed by a border of picot edging. Bullion-stitch rosebuds make extra-special embroidered accents. Designed by Gayle Bunn.

KNITTED MEASUREMENTS
■ Approx 33" x 37"/84cm x 94cm

MATERIALS
■ 9 1¾oz/50g balls (each approx 123yd/112m) of Patons® *Bumblebee* (cotton) in #2421 apple blossom (MC) ③
■ 6 balls in #2005 lily of the valley (A)
■ 2 balls in #2414 wild rose (B)
■ 1 ball in #2215 water lily (C)
■ Size 6 (4mm) circular needle 36"/90cm long *or size to obtain gauge*
■ Cable needle (cn)

GAUGE
22 sts and 30 rows to 4"/10cm over St st using size 6 (4mm) needles.
Take time to check gauge.

STITCH GLOSSARY
T3B
Slip next st to cn and hold to *back*, k2, then p1 from cn.
T3F
Slip next 2 sts to cn and hold to *front*, p1, then k2 from cn.
Tw2L
Slip next st to cn and hold to *front*, p1, then k1 tbl from cn.

Tw2R
Slip next st to cn and hold to *back*, k1 tbl, then p1 from cn.
C6F
Slip next 3 sts to cn and hold to *front*, k3, then k3 from cn.

INSTRUCTIONS
Center Section
With MC, cast on 199 sts. Work back and forth in rows as foll:

Row 1 (RS) K1, p1, *work row 1 of cable panel over 6 sts, p1, work row 1 of diamond panel over 19 sts, p1; rep from * 6 times more, work row 1 of cable panel over 6 sts, p1, k1.

Row 2 K2, *work row 2 of cable panel, k1, work row 2 of diamond panel, k1; rep from * 6 times more, work row 2 of cable panel, k2.

Row 3 K2, *work row 3 of cable panel, k1, work row 3 of diamond panel, k1; rep from * 6 times more, work row 3 of cable panel, k2.

Row 4 K1, p1, *work row 4 of cable panel, p1, work row 4 of diamond panel, p1; rep from * 6 times more, work row 4 of cable panel, p1, K1.

Cont in pats as established until 8 reps of diamond panel are complete (blanket measures approx 30"/76cm long), end with a WS row. Bind off.

FINISHING
Top or bottom edging
With RS facing and A, pick up and k 135

sts evenly across top edge of center section. P 1 row.

Next (inc) row K2, M1, k to last 2 sts, M1, k2. P 1 row.

Work border chart in St st, working inc rows as established and noting 6-st rep will be worked 22 times—159 sts.

Cont with A only.

Next row (fold line - RS) K1, *yo, k2tog; rep from * to end of row.

P1 row.

Next (dec) row K2, k2tog, k to last 4 sts, ssk, k2.

Rep last 2 rows 11 times more—135 sts. P 1 row. Bind off. Work in same way along bottom edge of center section.

Side edging

With RS of work facing and A, pick up and k 153 sts evenly along side edge of center section. Work as for top or bottom edging, working incs to 177 sts, then dec back to 153 sts and note 6-st rep of chart will be worked 25 times. Bind off. Work in same way along opposite side of center section.

Sew mitered corners of edgings tog. Fold edgings in half to WS along fold line and sew in position. Embroider bullion st roses with MC and B, then embroider chain st leaves with C.

Block to measurements.

Border chart

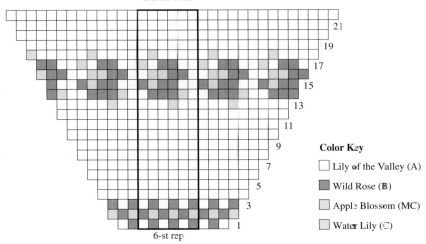

Color Key

- ☐ Lily of the Valley (A)
- ■ Wild Rose (B)
- ▨ Apple Blossom (MC)
- ☐ Water Lily (C)

6-st rep

Diamond Panel

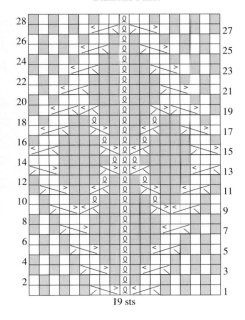

19 sts

Cable Panel

6 sts

Stitch Key

- ☐ K on RS, P on WS
- ▨ P on RS, K on WS
- Ⴍ K1 tbl on RS, p1 tbl on WS
- ⟍⟋ T3F
- ⟍⟋ T3B
- ⟍ TW2R
- ⟋ TW2L
- ⟍⟋ C6F

SAMPLER BLANKET
Family heirloom

■ ■ ■ ▶

Lace and texture are combined beautifully in this showpiece blanket. All squares are knit separately, then a simple crochet edge is worked around each square to make assembly easy. The lacy diamond border is worked in one long piece then sewn on for a delicate finish. Designed by Margarita Mejia.

KNITTED MEASUREMENTS
■ Approx 28" x 37"/71cm x 94cm

MATERIALS
■ 9 1¾oz/50g (each approx 170yd/158m) of Le Fibre Nobili® Plymouth Yarns *Merino* (wool) in #40-7 dark rose ②
■ One pair size 3 (3.25mm) needles *or size to obtain gauge*
■ Cable needle
■ Size D/3 (3.25mm) crochet hook for square edging

GAUGE
25 sts and 34 rows to 4"/10cm over St st using size 3 (3.25mm) needles.
Take time to check gauge.

STITCH GLOSSARY
MB
([K1, yo] twice, k1) all in next st, slip 4th, 3rd, 2nd and first sts separately over 5th st; bobble complete.

6-st RC
Sl 3 sts to cn and hold to *back*, k3, k3 from cn.

Sl 5 wyif
Sl next 5 sts knitwise, one at a time, with yarn in front of work.

BLANKET
Square A (make 5)
Cast on 34 sts.
Row 1 (RS) Knit.
Row 2 K8, [p2, k6] 3 times, k2.
Row 3 P8, [k2, p6] 3 times p2.
Row 4 Rep row 2.
Row 5 Knit.
Row 6 K4, [p2, k6] 3 times, p2, k4.
Row 7 P4, [k2, p6] 3 times, k2, p4.
Row 8 Rep row 6.
Rep rows 1-8 for basketweave pat until piece measures approx 5"/12.5cm ending with row 4 or 8 of pat. Bind off.

Square B (make 5)
Cast on 33 sts.
Row 1 (RS) Knit.
Row 2 and all WS rows Purl.
Row 3 K8, yo, sl 1, k2tog, psso. yo, k11, yo, sl 1, k2tog, psso, yo, k8.
Row 5 K6, k2tog, yo, k3, yo, ssk, k7, k2tog, yo, k3, yo, ssk, k6.
Row 7 K5, k2tog, yo, k5, yo, ssk, k5, k2tog, yo, k5, yo, ssk, k5.
Row 9 K4, k2tog, yo, k7, yo, ssk, k3, k2tog, yo, k7, yo, ssk, k4.
Row 11 K3, k2tog, yo, k9, yo, ssk, k1, k2tog, yo, k9, yo, ssk, k3.
Row 13 K2, k2tog, yo, k5, MB, k5, yo, sl 1, k2tog, psso, yo, k5, MB, k5, yo, ssk, k2.
Row 15 K4, yo, ssk, k7, k2tog, yo, k3, yo, ssk, k7, k2tog, yo, k4.

Row 17 [K5, yo, ssk, k5, k2tog, yo] twice, k5.

Row 19 K6, yo, ssk, k3, k2tog, yo, k7, yo, ssk, k3, k2tog, yo, k6.

Row 21 K7, yo, ssk, k1, k2tog, yo, k9, yo, ssk, k1, k2tog, yo, k7.

Row 23 K8, yo, sl 1, k2tog, psso, yo, k5, MB, k5, yo, sl 1, k2tog, psso, yo, k8.

Rows 25-44 Rep rows 5-22.

Row 45 Rep row 3.

Row 47 Knit.

Row 48 Purl.

Bind off.

Square C (make 4)

Cast on 36 sts.

Row 1 (RS) K2, p2, [k6, p2, k1, p2] twice, k6, p2, k2.

Row 2 and all WS rows K4, [p6, k5] twice, p6, k4.

Row 3 K2, p2, [6-st RC, p2, k1, p2] twice, 6-st RC, p2, k2.

Rows 5 and 7 Rep row 1.

Row 8 Rep row 2.

Rep rows 1-8 for cable pat until piece measures approx 5"/12.5cm ending with row 6 of pat. Bind off.

Square D (make 4)

Cast on 32 sts.

Row 1 (RS) K3, *k2tog, k5, yo, k1, yo, k2, ssk*, k2, rep from * to * once, k3.

Row 2 and all WS rows Purl.

Row 3 K3, *k2tog, k4, yo, k3, yo, k1, ssk*, k2, rep from * to * once, k3.

Row 5 K3, *k2tog, k3, yo, k5, yo, ssk*, k2, rep from * to * once, k3.

Row 7 K3, *k2tog, k2, yo, k1, yo, k5, ssk*, k2, rep from * to * once, k3.

Row 9 K3, *k2tog, k1, yo, k3, yo, k4, ssk*, k2, rep from * to * once, k3.

Row 11 K3, *k2tog, yo, k5, yo, k3, ssk*, k2, rep from * to * once, k3.

Row 12 Rep row 2.

Rep rows 1-12 for shell lace pat until square measures 5"/12.5cm ending with a WS row. Bind off.

Square E (make 4)

Cast on 34 sts.

Row 1 (WS) P.

Row 2 K1, [p1, k7] 4 times, k1.

Row 3 K1, [p6, k2] 4 times, k1.

Row 4 K1, [p3, k5] 4 times, k1.

Row 5 K1, [p4, k4] 4 times, k1.

Row 6 K1, [p5, k3] 4 times, k1.

Row 7 K1, [p2, k6] 4 times, k1.

Row 8 K1, [p7, k1] 4 times, k1.

Rep rows 1-8 for flag pat until piece measures approx 5"/12.5cm ending with row 1 of pat. Bind off.

Square F (make 4)

Cast on 35 sts.

Row 1 and all WS rows P.

Row 2 K3, *yo, ssk, k6; rep from * to end.

Row 4 K4, *yo, ssk, k3, k2tog, yo, k1; rep from * to last 7 sts, yo, ssk, k5.

Row 6 K5, *yo, ssk, k1, k2tog, yo, k3; rep from * to last 6 sts, yo, ssk, k4.

Row 8 K3, k2tog, *yo, k5, yo, sl 2 sts knitwise, k1, p2sso; rep from * to last 6 sts, yo, k6.

Row 10 K7, *yo, ssk, k6; rep from * to last

4 sts, yo, ssk, k2.

Row 12 K5, k2tog, *yo, k1, yo, ssk, k3, k2tog; rep from * to last 4 sts, yo, k4.

Row 14 K4, *k2tog, yo, k3, yo, ssk, k1; rep from * to last 7 sts, k2tog, yo, k5.

Row 16 K6, *yo, sl 2 sts knitwise, k1, p2sso, yo, k5; rep from * to last 5 sts, yo, k2tog, k3.

Rep rows 1-16 for rosebud lace pat until piece measures approx 5"/12.5cm ending with row 1 or 9 of pat. Bind off.

Square G (make 5)

Cast on 33 sts.

Row 1 (RS) K3, *yo, k2, p3, p3tog, p3, k2, yo, k1; rep from * to last 2 sts, k2.

Row 2 P6, k7, p7, k7, p6.

Row 3 K3, *k1, yo, k2, p2, p3tog, p2, k2, yo, k2; rep from * to last 2 sts, k2.

Row 4 P7, k5, p9, k5, p7.

Row 5 K5, *yo, k2, p1, p3tog, p1, k2, yo, k5; rep from * to end.

Row 6 P8, k3, p11, k3, p8.

Row 7 K6, *yo, k2, p3tog, k2, yo, k7; rep from *, end k6.

Row 8 P9, k1, p13, k1, p9.

Row 9 P2, p2tog, *p3, k2, yo, k1, yo, k2, p3 *, p3tog, rep from * to * once, p2tog, p2.

Row 10 K2, *k4, p7, k3; rep from * to last 3 sts, k3.

Row 11 P2, p2tog, *p2, k2, yo, k3, yo, k2, p2 *, p3tog, rep from * to * once, p2tog, p2.

Row 12 K2, *k3, p9, k2; rep from * to last 3 sts, k3.

Row 13 P2, p2tog, *p1, k2, yo, k5, yo, k2,

p1*, p3tog, rep from * to * once, p2tog, p2.

Row 14 K2, *k2, p11, k1; rep from * to last 3 sts, k3.

Row 15 P2, p2tog. *k2, yo, k7, yo, k2*, p3tog, rep from * to * once p2tog, p2.

Row 16 K2, *k1, p13; rep from * to last 3 sts, k3.

Rep rows 1-16 for wave pat until piece measures approx 5"/12.5cm ending with row 8 or 16 of pat. Bind off.

Square H (make 4)

Cast on 29 sts.

Row 1 (RS) Knit.

Rows 2, 4 and 6 Purl.

Rows 3, 5 and 7 K2, *k5, sl 5 wyif; rep from * to last 7 sts, k7.

Row 8 P9, *with RH needle in front of work, insert needle under 3 loose strands (from bottom to top) and p these 3 strands tog, p1, pass the p3tog over p1, p9; rep from * to end.

Rows 9, 11 and 13 K2, *sl 5 wyif, k5; rep from * to last 7 sts, sl 5 wyif, k2.

Rows 10 and 12 Purl.

Row 14 P4, *insert RH needle under 3 loose strands on RS of work, yo and draw up a lp, purl next st and sl lp just made over purl st, p9; rep from *, end last rep with p4. Rep rows 3-14 three times more for bow-tie pat.

Next row Knit.

Next row Purl.

Bind off.

FINISHING

With crochet hook, join yarn with sl st in

any corner and work sc evenly around outer edge of each square, working 3 sc in corners; join with sl st to first sc. Fasten off.

Sew squares together as shown in diagram.

LACE EDGING

Cast on 11 sts.

Row 1 (RS) Sl 1, k1 tbl, yo, k1, [yo, ssk] 3 times, k2.

Row 2 and all WS rows P.

Row 3 Sl 1, k1 tbl, yo, k3, [yo, ssk] 3 times, k1.

Row 5 Sl 1, k1 tbl, yo, k5, [yo, ssk] twice, k2.

Row 7 Sl 1, k1 tbl, yo, k7, [yo, ssk] twice, k1.

Row 9 Ssk, k1, yo, ssk, k3, [k2tog, yo] twice, k3.

Row 11 Ssk, k1, yo, ssk, k1, [k2tog, yo] 3 times, k2.

Row 13 Ssk, k1, yo, sl 1, k2tog, psso, (yo, k2tog) twice, yo, k3.

Row 15 Ssk, k2, [k2tog, yo] 3 times, k2.

Row 16 Purl.

Rep rows 1-16 for lace edging pat until piece measures length to fit around outer edge of blanket (approx 135"/343cm) ending with row 16 of pat. Bind off. Sew straight side of edging to blanket, gathering slightly at corners. Sew cast-on and bound-off edges tog.

Block to measurements.

H	F	E	B	G
B	A	D	C	F
H	G	E	D	A
D	H	F	A	G
A	G	E	B	C
F	C	G	H	B
A	B	C	D	E

35 Squares

ENTRELAC THROW
Beach blanket bingo

This fun-to-knit blanket—worked in a kaleidoscope of summer hues—features entrelac squares accented with contrast shades. Garter-stitch edging makes for a clean finish. Designed by Song Palmese.

KNITTED MEASUREMENTS
■ Approx 42" x 42"/106.5cm x 106.5cm

MATERIALS
■ 2 3½oz/100g balls (each approx 207yd/188m) of Lion Brand Yarn Company *Cotton Ease* (cotton/acrylic) each in #107 candy blue (A), #156 mint (B), #169 pistachio (C), #106 ice blue (D) and #700 sugar plum (E) (4)
■ One pair each size 6 (4mm) and size 9 (5.5mm) needles *or size to obtain gauge*

GAUGE
16 sts and 22 rows to 4"/10cm over St st using size 9 (5.5mm) needles.
Take time to check gauge.

Note
Blanket is worked in rounds, starting at center. Each square is picked up from the squares worked before it. Follow diagram for color placement. All squares on outer edges of Blanket have 2 sts at each edge worked in garter st.

STITCH GLOSSARY
CDD (centered double decrease)
Slip next 2 sts tog as if to k2tog, then knit next st; using tip of LH needle, pass 2 slipped sts over last knit st.

BLANKET
Square I
With smaller needles and first color, cast on 29 sts. K 1 row. Change to larger needles.
Row I K13, CDD, k to end.
Row 2 and all WS rows Purl.
Row 3 K12, CDD, k to end.
Row 5 K11, CDD, k to end.
Cont as established, working one fewer st before dec each row until 13 sts rem, end with RS facing. Cut first color. Change to second color and cont working established decs until 3 sts rem.
Next row (WS) Sl first 2 sts purlwise, p1, pass 2 slipped sts over last purl st. Fasten off.

Square 2
With smaller needles and first color, pick up and k 14 sts along edge of previous square, 1 st in top CDD of square, then cast on 14 sts—29 sts.
Complete as for square 1.

Square 3
With smaller needles and first color, cast on 14 sts, pick up 1 st in top CDD of square below, then pick up and k 14 sts along edge of previous square—29 sts.
Complete as for square 1.

Square 4
*With smaller needles and first color, pick

up and k 14 sts along edge of previous square, 1 st in top CDD of square below and 14 sts along edge of next previous square—29 sts.*
Complete as for square 1.

Foll diagram for color placement, work all squares beg with square 1 and picking up all foll squares from previously worked ones.

Squares on outer edges

Work as for square 4, noting all WS rows will be worked as foll: k2, purl to last 2 sts, k2.

FINISHING

Block lightly to measurements.

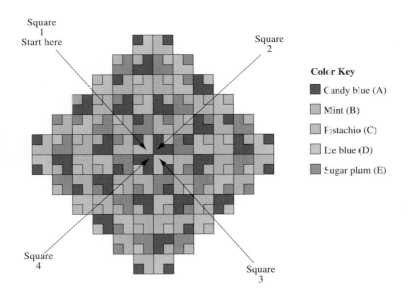

Square 1 Start here

Square 2

Square 4

Square 3

Color Key

■ Candy blue (A)
□ Mint (B)
□ Pistachio (C)
□ Ice blue (D)
■ Sugar plum (E)

■■■□

A bold cable lattice pattern offers ample textural interest to this snuggle-friendly blanket. Designed by Katherine Fedewa, it makes an exquisite addition to any nursery.

KNITTED MEASUREMENTS
■ Approx 26" x 30"/66cm x 76cm

MATERIALS
■ 7 1¾oz/50g balls (each approx 76yd/70m) of Stahl Wolle/Skacel Collection *Winter-Cotton* (cotton/acrylic) in #9910 grey (MC) **(4)**
■ 2 balls in #9914 red (CC)
■ Size 10 (6mm) circular needle, 36"/90cm long or *size to obtain gauge*
■ Cable needle (cn)

GAUGE
18 sts and 23 rows to 5"/12.5cm over diamond cable pat using size 10 (6mm) needles. *Take time to check gauge.*

STITCH GLOSSARY
4-st LC Slip next 2 sts to cn and hold to *front*, k next 2 sts, k2 from cn.

3-st LPC Slip next 2 sts to cn and hold to *front*, p next st, k2 from cn.

3-st RPC Slip next st to cn and hold to *back*, k next 2 sts, p1 from cn.

DIAMOND CABLE PATTERN
(Multiple of 12 sts)

Row 1 (RS) K2, p8, *4-st LC, p8; rep from * to last 2 sts, k2.

Row 2 (WS) P2, k8, *p4, k8; rep from * to last 2 sts, p2.

Row 3 K2, p8, *k4, p8; rep from * to last 2 sts, k2.

Row 4 Rep row 2.

Row 5 Rep row 1.

Row 6 Rep row 2.

Row 7 *3-st LPC, p6, 3-st RPC; rep from * to end.

Row 8 K1, p2, k6, p2, *k2, p2, k6, p2; rep from * to last st, k1.

Row 9 P1, 3-st LPC, p4, 3-st RPC, *p2, 3-st LPC, p4, 3-st RPC; rep from * to last st, p1.

Row 10 K2, p2, *k4, p2; rep from * to last 2 sts, k2.

Row 11 P2, 3-st LPC, p2, 3-st RPC, *p4, 3-st LPC, p2, 3-st RPC; rep from * to last 2 sts, p2.

Row 12 K3, p2, k2, p2, *k4, p2, k2, p2; rep from * to last 3 sts, k3.

Row 13 P3, 3-st LPC, 3-st RPC, *p6, 3-st LPC, 3-st RPC; rep from * to last 3 sts, p3.

Row 14 K4, p4, *k8, p4; rep from * to last 4 sts, k4.

Row 15 P4, 4-st LC, *p8, 4-st LC; rep from * to last 4 sts, p4.

Row 16 Rep row 14.

Row 17 P4, k4, *p8, k4; rep from * to last 4 sts, p4.

Row 18 Rep row 14.

Row 19 Rep row 15.

Row 20 Rep row 14.

Row 21 P3, 3-st RPC, 3-st LPC, *p6, 3-st RPC, 3-st LPC; rep from * to last 3 sts, p3.

Row 22 Rep row 12.

Row 23 P2, 3-st RPC, p2, 3-st LPC, *p4, 3-st RPC, p2, 3-st LPC; rep from * to last 2 sts, p2.

Row 24 Rep row 10.

Row 25 P1, 3-st RPC, p4, 3-st LPC, *p2, 3-st RPC, p4, 3-st LPC; rep from * to last st, p1.

Row 26 Rep row 8.

Row 27 *3-st RPC, p6, 3-st LPC; rep from * to end.

Row 28 Rep row 2.

Rep rows 1-28 for diamond cable pat.

BLANKET

With MC, cast on 108 sts. Work rows 1-28 of diamond cable pat 5 times, then rep rows 1 to 20 once. Piece measures approx 28"/71cm. Do *not* bind off. Cut MC.

BORDER

Row 1 With CC, k5, *k2tog, k10; rep from * to last 7 sts, k2tog, k5—99 sts.

Rows 2-6 Knit.

Bind off all sts, keeping last loop on needle (counts as first st for next border edge).

Note

Border is worked one edge at a time, counterclockwise around the blanket.

With RS facing, pick up and k 3 sts along left edge of border just worked and 120 sts down side edge of blanket—124 sts.

Row 2 Knit.

Row 3 Sl 1 st purlwise, k to end.

Row 4 Knit.

Row 5 Sl 1 st purlwise, k to end.

Row 6 Knit.

Bind off all sts, keeping last loop on needle (counts as first st for next border edge).

With RS facing, pick up and k 3 sts along left edge of border just worked and 99 sts along cast-on edge of blanket—103 sts.

Row 2 Knit.

Row 3 Sl 1 st purlwise, k to end.

Row 4 Knit.

Row 5 Sl 1 st purlwise, k to end.

Row 6 Knit.

Bind off all sts, keeping last loop on needle (counts as first st for next border edge).

With RS facing, pick up and k 3 sts along left edge of border just worked,120 sts up side of blanket and 4 sts along right edge of first border—128 sts.

Rows 2-6 Sl 1 st purlwise, k to end.

Bind off.

FINISHING

Lightly block blanket to measurements.

■■■▭

Baby boys and girls will delight in these comical ducks with flapping bills. Simple stripes are edged with garter stitch. Designed by Amy Bahrt.

Note
When changing colors, twist yarns on WS to prevent holes in work. Use a separate bobbin of yarn for each block of color.

STRIPE PATTERN
Row 1 K5 A, k133 MC, k5 A.
Row 2 K5 A, P133 MC, k5 A.
Rows 3 and 4 Rep rows 1 and 2.
Row 5 With A, knit.
Row 6 With A, k5, p to last 5 sts, k5.
Rows 7 and 8 Rep rows 5 and 6.

Rep rows 1-8 for stripe pat.

BLANKET
With A, cast on 143 sts. Work 8 rows in garter st. Work in stripe pat until blanket measures approx 29"/74cm ending on row 8 of pat.
Row 1 K5 A, k133 MC, k5 A.
Row 2 K5 A, p133 with MC, k5 A.
Rep last 2 rows once more, then row 1 once.

Place ducks
Next row (WS) K5 A, *p22 MC, work row 1 of chart over next 15 sts; rep from * twice more, p22 MC, k5 A.
Cont in pats as established through row 26 of chart.
Row 1 (WS) K5 A, p133 MC, k5 A.
Row 2 K5 A, k133 MC, k5 A.
Rep last 2 rows once more, then row 1 once.
With A, work 8 rows garter st. Bind off.

FINISHING
Embroidery
With MC, using french knots, embroider duck's eyes as indicated on chart. With MC, using chain st, embroider duck's wings as indicated on chart.

Duck bill (make 3)
With B, cast on 4 sts.
Row 1 (RS) Inc 1 st in first st, k1, inc 1 st in next st, k1—6 sts.
Work 7 more rows in St st. Bind off. With

B, embroider chain st around outer edge of bill. Sew bound-off edge in place on duck as indicated on chart.

Block blanket to measurements.

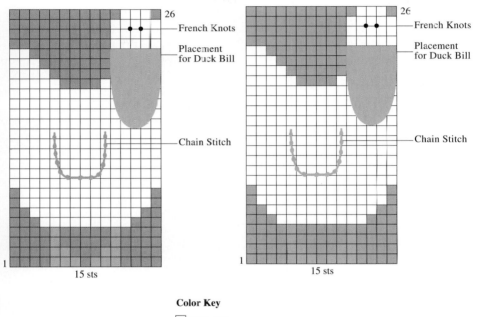

26 — French Knots

Placement for Duck Bill

Chain Stitch

1

15 sts

26 — French Knots

Placement for Duck Bill

Chain Stitch

1

15 sts

Color Key

☐ White(A)

▨ Yellow (B)

▨ Blue (MC)
or
▨ Rose (MC)

Wish upon a star

■■■□

A spirited baby throw worked from separate diamonds are sewn together in a tile pattern. Alternating diamonds in star-stitch texture create an eye-catching effect. Designed by Gayle Bunn.

KNITTED MEASUREMENTS
■ Approx 32" x 38"/81.5cm x 96.5cm

MATERIALS
■ 7 1¾oz/50g balls (each approx 150yd/139m) Patons *Look at Me* (acrylic/nylon) in #6717 fun 'n games (MC) ③
■ 4 balls each of #6351 lagoon (A) and #6360 peacock (B)
■ One pair size 7 (4.5mm) needles *or size to obtain gauge*

GAUGE
25 sts and 30 rows = 4"/10cm over pat using size 7 (4.5mm) needles.
Take time to check gauge.

STITCH GLOSSARY
Star = P3tog, but do not slip sts off needle, yo and p same 3 sts tog again, slip sts off needle.

BLANKET
Diamond A (make 20)
With A, cast on 3 sts.
Row 1 (RS) K3.
Row 2 P3.
Row 3 With B, [k1, M1] twice, k1—5 sts.
Row 4 P5.

Row 5 With A, k1, M1, k3, M1, k1—7 sts.
Row 6 P1, k1, Star, k1, p1.
Row 7 With B, k1, M1, k5, M1, k1—9 sts.
Row 8 P1, Star, k1, Star, p1.
Row 9 With A, k1, M1, k7, M1, K1—11 sts.
Row 10 P3, k1, Star, k1, p3.
Row 11 With B, k1, M1, k9, M1, k1—13 sts.
Row 12 P2, [k1, Star] twice, k1, p2.
Row 13 With A, k1, M1, k11, M1, k1—15 sts.
Row 14 P1, [k1, Star] 3 times, k1, p1.
Row 15 With B, k1, M1, k13, M1, k1—17 sts.
Row 16 P1, [Star, k1] 3 times, Star, p1.
Row 17 With A, k1, M1, k15, M1, k1—19 sts.
Row 18 P3, [k1, Star] 3 times, k1, p3.
Row 19 With B, k1, M1, k17, M1, k1—21 sts.
Row 20 P2, [k1, Star] 4 times, k1, p2.
Row 21 With A, k1, M1, k19, M1, k1—23 sts.
Row 22 P1, [k1, Star] 5 times, k1, p1.
Row 23 With B, k1, M1, k21, M1, k1—25 sts.
Row 24 P1, [Star, k1] 5 times, Star, p1.
Row 25 With A, k1, M1, k23, M1, k1—27 sts.
Row 26 P3, [k1, Star] 5 times, k1, p3.
Row 27 With B, k1, M1, k25, M1, k1—29 sts.
Row 28 P2, [k1, Star] 6 times, k1, P2.
Row 29 With A, k1, M1, k27, M1, k1—31 sts.
Row 30 P1, k1, [Star, k1] 7 times, p1.

Row 31 With B, k1, M1, k29, M1, k1—33 sts.

Row 32 P1, [Star, k1] 7 times, Star, p1.

Row 33 With B, k1, ssk, k27, k2tog, k1—31 sts.

Row 34 Rep row 30.

Row 35 With A, k1, ssk, k25, k2tog, k1—29 sts.

Row 36 Rep row 28.

Row 37 With B, k1, ssk, k23, k2tog, k1—27 sts.

Row 38 Rep row 26.

Row 39 With A, k1, ssk, k21, k2tog, k1—25 sts.

Row 40 Rep row 24.

Row 41 With B, k1, ssk, k19, k2tog, K1—23 sts.

Row 42 Rep row 22.

Row 43 With A, k1, ssk, k17, k2tog, k1—21 sts.

Row 44 Rep row 20.

Row 45 With B, k1, ssk, k15, k2tog, k1—19 sts.

Row 46 Rep row 18.

Row 47 With A, k1, ssk, k13, k2tog, k1—17 sts.

Row 48 Rep row 16.

Row 49 With B, k1, ssk, k11, k2tog, k1—15 sts.

Row 50 Rep row 14.

Row 51 With A, k1, ssk, k9, k2tog, k1—13 sts.

Row 52 Rep row 12.

Row 53 With B, k1, ssk, k7, k2tog, k1—11 sts.

Row 54 Rep row 10.

Row 55 With A, k1, ssk, k5, k2tog, k1—9 sts.

Row 56 Rep row 8.

Row 57 With B, k1, ssk, k3, k2tog, k1—7 sts.

Row 58 Rep row 6.

Row 59 With A, k1, ssk, k1, k2tog, k1—5 sts.

Row 60 P5.

Row 61 With B, k1, sl 1, k2tog, psso, k1—3 sts.

Row 63 P3tog. Fasten off.

Diamond B (make 30)

With MC, work as for diamond A, omitting all reference to color changes.

FINISHING

Sew diamonds tog into 6 strips of diamond B (5 diamonds long) alternating with 5 strips of diamond A (4 diamonds long). Block blanket to measurements.

With MC, make 12 tassels and sew to points at each end of blanket.

■■■□

Go graphic—bold blocks come together and add excitement to this garter-stitched intarsia blanket. Designed by Kennita Tully.

KNITTED MEASUREMENTS
■ Approx 35" x 35"/89cm x 89cm

MATERIALS
■ 3 3½oz/100g skeins (each approx 215yd/197m) of Brown Sheep Co. *Cotton Fleece* (cotton/wool) each in #CW-005 cavern (A) and #CW-100 cottonball (B) (4️)
■ 1 skein in #CW-201 barn red (C)
■ One size 7 (4.5mm) circular needle 29"/74cm long *or size to obtain gauge*

GAUGE
17 sts and 34 rows to 4"/10cm over garter st using size 7 (4.5mm) needles.

Take time to check gauge.

Notes
1 When changing colors, twist yarns on WS to prevent holes in work. Use a separate bobbin of yarn for each block of color.
2 Each square of color chart represents 1 st and 2 rows.

BLANKET
[Cast on 25 sts A, cast on 25 sts B] 3 times —150 sts. Working back and forth in rows, follow diagram for color placement and work all charts in garter st. Bind off.

FINISHING
Block blanket to measurements.

PLACEMENT DIAGRAM

D	C	B	C	B	A
C	I	C	B	E	B
B	C	H	G	B	C
C	B	G	H	C	B
B	E	B	C	I	C
A	B	C	B	C	D

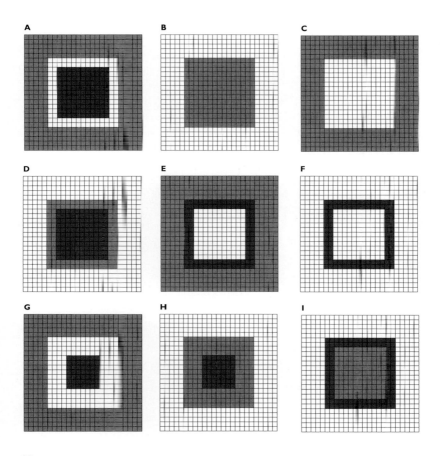

Note

Each square of chart represents 1 st and 2 rows. Therefore,
each chart is 25 sts and 50 rows.

■■■ ▭

A striking jewel-toned palette lends drama to this nursery gem. The garter-stitched squares are picked up along the sides of adjoining squares to speed up finishing. Designed by Wendy Bergman.

KNITTED MEASUREMENTS
■ Approx 28" x 28'/71cm x 71cm

MATERIALS
■ 2 1¾oz/50g balls (each approx 98yd/90m) of Karabella Yarn *Aurora 8* (wool) each in #1148 black (A), #7 red (B), #8 orange (C), #1778 gold (D), #716 green (E), #1556 blue (F), #3 purple (G), #2 burgundy (H) (3)
■ One pair size 7 (4.5mm) double pointed needles *or size to obtain gauge*

GAUGE
One square to 2¾"/7cm using size 7 (4.5mm) needles.
Take time to check gauge.

Note
Begin each square with color shown in bottom right corner (first color). Carry colors when not in use up side of work. Diagram shows ¼ of blanket.

STITCH GLOSSARY
Square
For first square, with first color, cast on 25 sts.

For squares joined to 1 side, with first color cast on 12 sts, then with RS facing, pick up and k 13 sts across side of adjoining square.

For squares joined to 2 sides, with RS facing, pick up and k 12 sts along side of 1 square, 1 st in corner, then 12 sts up side of other square.

Row 1 (WS) K to last st, p1.
Change to second color.
Row 2 Sl 1, k10, sl 1, k2tog, psso, k10, p1—23 sts.
Row 3 Sl 1, k to last st, p1.
Change to first color.
Row 4 Sl 1, k9, sl 1, k2tog psso, k9, p1—21 sts.
Row 5 Sl 1, k to last st, p1
Change to second color.
Row 6 Sl 1, k8, sl 1, k2tog, psso, k8, p1—19 sts.
Row 7 Sl 1, k to last st, p1.
Cont in this way, working 2 rows in each color and dec 2 sts every other row until 3 sts rem.
Next row With second color, sl 1, k1, p1.
Next row Sl 1, k2tog, psso. Fasten off.

BLANKET
Follow diagram for color placement and begin with square in top left corner. When 25 squares of first ¼ are complete, repeat this ¼ 3 times more, rotating each repeat 90° to the right. There will be 4 squares worked in A and E joined at center.

Block lightly to measurements.

Edging

With A, cast on 5 sts.

K3, p2tog, bring yarn to back, pick up and k 1 st (from ridge) on side edge of blanket. Slide sts to to other end of double pointed needle; rep from * around blanket working 3 times into each corner. Bind off. Sew bound-off and cast-on edges tog.

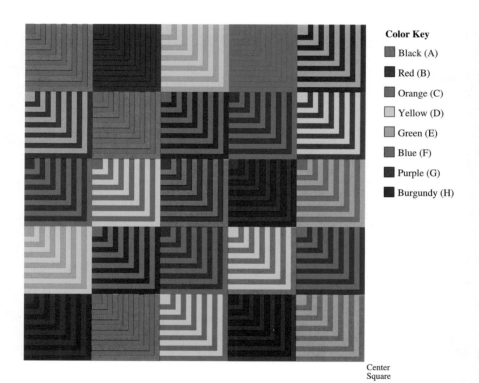

Color Key

Black (A)
Red (B)
Orange (C)
Yellow (D)
Green (E)
Blue (F)
Purple (G)
Burgundy (H)

Center
Square

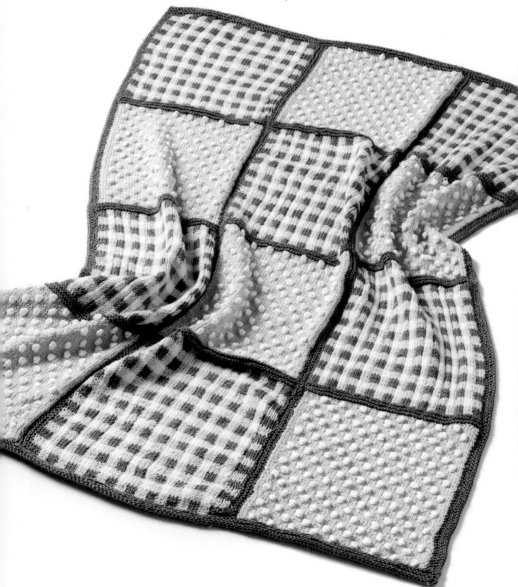

Textured polka dots and fanciful gingham team up in this crib-sized blanket that is worked in three strips. Garter-stitch trim borders provide a clean finish and striking contrast. Designed by Gayle Bunn.

■ Approx 33" x 46"/84cm x 117cm

■ 6 1¾oz/50g balls (each approx 136yd/125m) of Patons® *Grace* (cotton) in #60104 azure (MC) ⊛
■ 5 balls each in #60603 apricot (A) and #60005 snow (B)
■ 4 balls in #60130 sky (C)
■ One pair of size 5 (3.75mm) needles *or size to obtain gauge*
■ Size 5 (3.75mm) circular needle 36"/90cm long

24 sts and 32 rows to 4"/10 cm over St st using size 5 (3.75mm) needles.
Take time to check gauge.

Note
Throw is worked in 3 strips which are edged in garter stitch, then sewn together. Garter stitch edging on top and bottom edges is worked after strips are sewn together.

Make Bobble (MB)

With B, ([k1, p1] 3 times, k1) all in next st, slip 6th, 5th, 4th, 3rd, 2nd and first sts separately over 7th st—1 st rem. Bobble complete.

Row 1 (RS) With A, knit.
Row 2 and all WS rows With A, purl.
Row 3 K4 A, with B, MB, *k5 A, with B, MB; rep from * to last 4 sts, k4 A.
Row 5 With A, knit.
Row 7 K7 A, with B, MB, *k5 A, with B, MB; rep from * to last 7 sts, k7 A.
Row 8 With A, purl.
Rep rows 1-8 for dot pat.

Row 1 (RS) K4 MC, *k3 C, k3 MC; rep from * to last 7 sts, k3 C, k4 MC.
Row 2 P4 MC, *p3 C, p3 MC; rep from * to last 7 sts, p3 C, p4 MC.
Rows 3 and 4 Rep rows 1 and 2.
Row 5 K4 C, *k3 B, k3 C; rep from * to last 7 sts, k3 B, k4 C.
Row 6 P4 C, *p3 B, p3 C; rep from * to last 7 sts, p3 B, p4 C.
Rows 7 and 8 Rep Rows 5 and 6.
Rep rows 1-8 for check pat.

Strips 1 and 3
With A and pair of needles, cast on 57 sts.
**Work 72 rows in dot pat.
With MC, work 6 rows garter st, inc 2 sts evenly across last row—59 sts.
Work 68 rows in check pat, dec 2 sts even-

ly across last row—57 sts.**
With MC, work 6 rows garter st.
Rep from ** to ** once. With MC, bind off.

Strip 2

**With MC, cast on 59 sts.
Work 68 rows in check pat, dec 2 sts
evenly across last row—57 sts.
With MC, work 6 rows garter st.
Work 72 rows in dot pat.**
With MC, work 6 rows garter st, inc 2 sts
evenly across last row—59 sts.
Rep from ** to ** once more. With A,
bind off.

FINISHING
Block to measurements.

Strip edging
(Worked on both side edges of strip 1 and
right side edge only of strips 2 and 3.)
With RS facing, MC and circular needle,
pick up and k 212 sts evenly along side
edge of strip. Work 5 rows garter st. Bind off.
Sew strips tog.

TOP AND BOTTOM EDGING
With RS facing, MC and circular needle,
pick up and k 152 sts across top edge
of throw. Work 5 rows garter st. Bind
off. Work in same way along bottom edge
of throw.

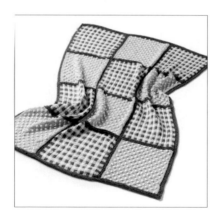

This snazzy blanket boasts individual triangles stitched in fresh shades of green. Stockinette stitch alternates with reverse stockinette for subtle texture. A matching toy block takes baby from naptime to playtime. Designed by Teva Durham.

KNITTED MEASUREMENTS
■ Approx 21" x 32"/53.5cm x 81.5cm (point to point, excluding tassels)

MATERIALS
■ 3 each 1¾oz/50g (each approx 189yd/175m) of Dale of Norway *Baby Wool* (wool) in #8523 lime green (A) and #9013 light lime green (B) **(2)**
■ One pair size 5 (3.75mm) needles *or size to obtain gauge*
■ Optional toy block requires small quantity of fiberfill stuffing

GAUGE
20 sts and 28 rows to 4"/10cm over St st using size 5 (3.75mm) needles.
Take time to check gauge.

Note
When changing colors, twist yarns on WS to prevent holes in work. Use a separate bobbin of yarn for each block of color.

BLANKET
Triangle A (make 18)
With A, cast on 33 sts. Work chart 1 through row 48. Fasten off.

Triangle B (make 18)
With B, cast on 33 sts. Work chart 2 through row 48. Fasten off.

FINISHING
Sew triangles tog into 4 strips 9 triangles long, alternating triangle A with triangle B as shown. Make 6 tassels using A and B tog and sew to each point of blanket.

Block lightly to measurements.

TOY BLOCK
Make 3 triangle A and 1 triangle B as for blanket. Use 1 triangle A as base and sew rem 3 triangles to each side to form a cone shape, leaving 1 side open to insert fiberfill stuffing. Stuff firmly. Sew opening closed.

Chart 1

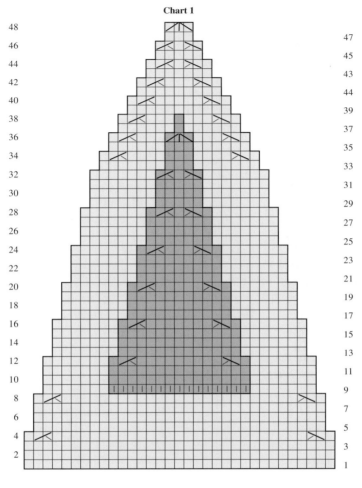

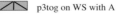

Stitch Key

- ☐ Rev St st with B
- ■ St st with A
- p2tog tbl on RS, ssk on WS with B
- p2tog on RS, k2tog on WS with B
- ssk on RS, p2tog tbl on WS with A
- k2tog on RS, p2tog on WS with A
- SK2P on WS with B
- p3tog on WS with A
- K on RS with A

Chart 2

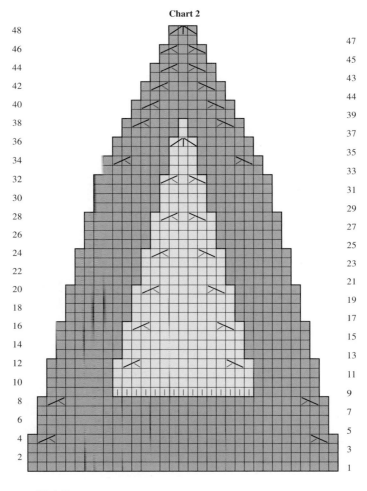

Stitch Key

Rev St st with B

St st with A

p2tog tbl or RS, ssk on WS with B

p2tog on RS, k2tog on WS with B

ssk on RS, p2tog tbl on WS with A

k2tog on RS, p2tog on WS with A

SK2P on WS with B

p3tog on WS with A

K on RS with B

Garter-stitched panels highlight the rich autumnal shades in this luxurious blanket. Matching terra-cotta tassels accent the ends. Designed by Veronica Manno.

KNITTED MEASUREMENTS
■ Approx 26" x 35"/65cm x 89cm

MATERIALS
■ 6 3½oz/100g hanks (each approx 108yd/100m) Colinette Yarns Unique Kolours *Isis* (viscose) in #102 pierrot (A)
■ Small amount of worsted weight yarn in coordinating solid color for tassels (B)
■ One pair size 11 (8mm) needles *or size to obtain gauge*

GAUGE
10 sts and 19 rows to 4"/10cm over garter st using size 11 (8mm) needles.
Take time to check gauge.

BLANKET
Strip (make 6)
With A, cast on 11 sts and work in garter st for 35"/89cm. Bind off.

FINISHING
Sew strips together. With B, make 14 tassels and attach to ends as shown in photograph.

Lightly block blanket to measurements.

A sampler blanket of knit and purl textures in fun shades makes for a great project to knit on-the-go. Each square is worked separately then joined into a patchwork design. Designed by Sandi Prosser.

KNITTED MEASUREMENTS

■ Approx 32" x 38"/5 cm x 96.5cm

MATERIALS

■ 1 6oz/170g skeins (each approx 509yd/465m) of Coats and Clark *TLC Baby* (acrylic) each in #7812 sky blue (MC), #7221 banana (A), #7624 lime (B) (3)

■ One pair size 6 (4mm) needles *or size to obtain gauge*

GAUGE

22 sts and 30 rows to 4"/10cm over St st using size 6 (4mm) needles.
Take time to check gauge.

Notes

1 Each square measures approx 6"/15cm square.

2 Follow diagram for color and stitch used for each square.

GARTER STITCH SQUARE

With MC, cast on 34 sts. Work in garter st until piece measures 6"/15cm. Bind off.

GARTER CHECKS SQUARE

With MC, cast on 35 sts.

Row 1 (RS) K5, *p5, k5; rep from * to end.

Row 2 Purl.

Rows 3 and 4 Rep rows 1 and 2.

Row 5 Rep row 1.

Row 6 K5, *p5, k5; rep from * to end.

Row 7 Knit.

Rows 8 and 9 Rep rows 6 and 7.

Row 10 Rep row 6.

Rep rows 1-10 4 times more, then rep rows 1-5 once. Bind off.

GARTER TRIANGLES SQUARE

With A, cast on 33 sts.

Row 1 (RS) P1, *k7, p1. rep from * to end.

Row 2 and all WS rows Purl.

Row 3 P2, *k5, p3; rep from * to last 7 sts, k5, p2.

Row 5 P3, *k3, p5; rep from * to last 6 sts, k3, p3.

Row 7 P4, *k1, p7; rep from * to last 5 sts, k1, p4.

Row 9 K4, *p1, k7; rep from * to last 5 sts, p1, k4.

Row 11 K3, *p3, k5; rep from * to last 6 sts, p3, k3.

Row 13 K2, *p5, k3; rep from * to last 7 sts, p5, k2.

Row 15 K1, *p7, k1; rep from * to end of row.

Row 16 Purl.

Rep rows 1-16 twice more, then rep rows 1-8 once. Bind off.

DOUBLE FLECK SQUARE

With A, cast on 34 sts.
Row 1 (RS) Knit.
Row 2 P4, *k2, p4; rep from * to end.
Row 3 Knit.
Row 4 P1, *k2, p4; rep from * to last 3 sts, k2, p1.
Rep rows 1-4 for double fleck pat until piece measures 6"/15cm. Bind off.

TEXTURED RIB SQUARE

With B, cast on 35 sts.
Row 1 (RS) Knit.
Row 2 K3, *p1, k3; rep from * to end.
Rows 3 and 4 Rep rows 1 and 2.
Row 5 Knit.
Row 6 K1, p1, *k3, p1; rep from *, end k1.
Rows 7 and 8 Rep rows 5 and 6.
Rep rows 1-8 for textured rib pat until piece measures 6"/15cm. Bind off.

ZIG ZAG SQUARE

With B, cast on 36 sts.
Row 1 (RS) *K3, p3; rep from * to end.
Row 2 and all WS rows Purl.
Row 3 P1, *k3, p3; rep from * to last 5 sts, k3, p2.
Row 5 P2, *k3, p3; rep from * to last 4 sts, k3, p1.

Row 7 *P3, k3; rep from * to end.
Row 9 Rep row 5.
Row 11 Rep row 3.
Row 12 P.
Rep rows 1-12 for zig zag pat until piece measures 6"/15cm. Bind off.

FINISHING

Sew squares tog as shown in diagram.
Top or bottom edging
With RS facing and MC, pick up and k 150 sts evenly across top edge of blanket.
Next row (WS) Knit.
Next 2 rows With A, knit.
Next 2 rows With B, knit.
Next row With MC, knit.
With MC, bind off.
Work in same way along bottom edge of blanket.

Side edging
With RS of work facing and MC, pick up and k 186 sts evenly along side edge of blanket. Work as for top or bottom edging. Work in same way along opposite side of blanket.

Block to measurements.

Garter Triangles	Garter Stitch	Zig Zag	Double Fleck	Garter Checks
Zig Zag	Double Fleck	Garter Checks	Textured Rib	Garter Triangles
Garter Checks	Textured Rib	Garter Triangles	Garter Stitch	Zig Zag
Garter Triangles	Garter Stitch	Zig Zag	Double Fleck	Garter Checks
Zig Zag	Double Fleck	Garter Checks	Textured Rib	Garter Triangles
Garter Checks	Textured Rib	Garter Triangles	Garter Stitch	Zig Zag

CRAZY STRIPES BLANKET

Color my world

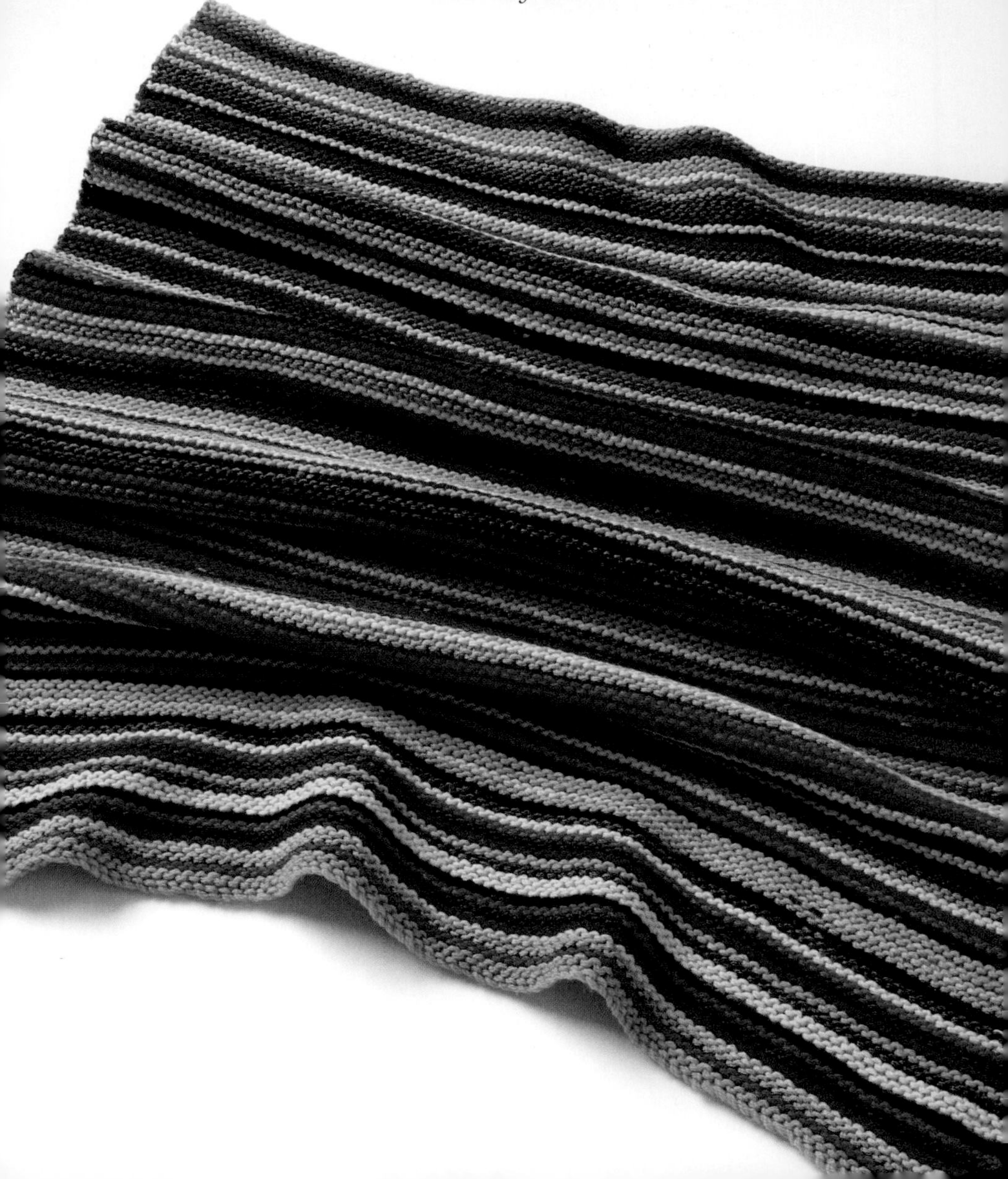

A vibrant palette offers cheer to an easy-to-knit, garter-stitched blanket that's perfect for the stroller or car seat. Designed by Veronica Manno.

KNITTED MEASUREMENTS
- Approx 23" x 28"/58.5cm x 71cm

MATERIALS
- 1   1¾oz/50g hanks (each approx 114yd/105m) Koigu Wool Design *Kersti* (wool) each in #K1100 red (A), #1520 green (B), #K1190 orange (C), #K1002 royal (D), #K1005 lt blue (E), #K1521 lime (F), #K2409 black (G), #K1016 purple (H) #K2130 turquoise (I) ▣
- One size 7 (4.5mm) circular needle, 32"/80cm long *or size to obtain gauge*

GAUGE
20 sts and 38 rows to 4"/10cm over garter st using size 7 (4.5mm) needle.
Take time to check gauge.

BLANKET
With I, cast on 109 sts. Work 2 row stripes in garter st, using all colors as desired. If desired, approx every 20 rows, work 4 rows in garter st with one shade. When blanket measures approx 28"/71cm from beg, bind off.

FINISHING
Weave in all ends. Block blanket to measurements.

SHELL STITCH COVERLET
Confetti colors

■■■☐

Delicate openwork shells are accented with hints of color in this light and lacy blanket. Garter-stitch borders are knit in for no-fuss self-finishing. Designed by Kathy Hightower.

KNITTED MEASUREMENTS
■ Approx 26" x 31 '/66cm x 78.5cm

MATERIALS
■ 6 1¾oz/50g (each approx 193yd/178m) of Sesia/LBUSA *Sesia Baby Print* (cotton) in #657 yellow 🔳3🔳
■ One pair size 3 (3.25mm) needles or *size to obtain gauge*

GAUGE
23 sts and 36 rows to 4"/10cm over shell pat using size 3 (3.25mm) needles.

SHELL PATTERN

Note
St counts vary on each row. Count sts after rows 7 and 8 only.
Row I (RS) K3, *yo, k8, yo, k1; rep from * to last 3 sts, yo, k3.
Row 2 K4, *p8, k3; rep from * to last st, k1.
Row 3 K4, *yo, k8, yo, k3; rep from * to last st, k1.
Row 4 K5, *p8, k5; rep from * to end.
Row 5 K5, *yo, k8, yo, k5; rep from * to end.
Row 6 K6, *p8, k7; rep from * to last 14 sts, p8, k6.
Row 7 K6, *k4tog tbl, k4tog, k7. rep from * to last 14 sts, k4tog tbl, k4tog, k6.
Row 8 Knit.
Rep rows 1-8 for shell pat.

BLANKET
Cast on 149 sts.
K 4 rows.
Work in shell pat until piece measures approx 30½"/77.5cm from beg, end with row 8 of pat.
K 4 rows. Bind off loosely.

FINISHING
Block to measurements.

Simple garter-stitched stripes in muted grey tones create the fine lines of this cuddly blanket. The sawtooth edging, worked in short rows, adds a touch of whimsy. Designed by Lora Steil.

KNITTED MEASUREMENTS
■ Approx 25" x 32"/63.5cm x 81.5cm (excluding edging)

MATERIALS
■ 3 1¾oz/50g hanks (each approx 142yd/132m) of Classic Elite Yarn *03 Tweed* (wool) each in #492 dk grey (A) and #489 lt grey (B) (3)
■ 1 hank each in #474 orange (C), #483 blue (D), #479 red (E) and #486 green (F).
■ One size 5 (3.75mm) circular needle, 29"/74cm long
■ One pair size 5 (3.75mm) needles *or size to obtain gauge*

GAUGE
20 sts and 42 rows to 4"/10cm over garter st using size 5 (3.75mm) needles.
Take time to check gauge.

BLANKET
With circular needle and A, cast on 125 sts. K 1 row.
Rows 1 and 2 With B, knit.
Rows 3 and 4 With A, knit.
Rep last 4 rows for stripe pat until blanket measures 32"/81.5cm from beg, end with 4th row of stripe pat.

Next row With B, knit.
With B, bind off.

FINISHING
Note
When picking up sts for edging, there will be 16 triangles worked on each side edge and 12 triangles worked across top or bottom edges. Skip rows on side edges or sts on top or bottom edges when picking up sts, as necessary, to ensure triangles lie flat.

Edging
With RS facing, pair of needles and C, beg at bottom right corner, pick up and k 1 st in corner of blanket.
*Next row Turn, k1.
Next row Turn, k1, then pick up and k 1 st in side of blanket.
Next row Turn, k2.
Next row Turn, k2, then pick up and k 1 st in side of blanket.
Next row Turn, k3.
Cont in this way, picking up 1 st in side of blanket on next and every other row, until there are 8 sts on needle.
Next row Turn, k8.
Bind off 8 sts, then pick up and k 1 st in side of blanket with D and bind off rem loop of C over D st.*
Rep from * to * around blanket in color sequence C, D, E and F.

Block to measurements.

RESOURCES

*Write to the yarn
companies listed below for
purchasing and mail-order
information.*

ANNY BLATT
7796 Boardwalk
Brighton, MI 48116

ARTFUL YARNS
distributed by
JCA

BERROCO,INC.
P. O. Box 367
Uxbridge, MA 01569

BROWN SHEEP CO.
100662 County Road 16
Mitchell, NE 69357

CLASSIC ELITE YARNS
300A Jackson Street
Lowell, MA 01852

COATS AND CLARK, INC.
Attn: Consumer Service
PO Box 12229
Greenville, SC 29612-0229

COLINETTE YARNS
distributed by
Unique Kolours

DALE OF NORWAY
N16 W23390 Stoneridge
Drive, Suite A
Waukesha, WI 53188

DEBBIE BLISS
distributed by
KFI

JCA
35 Scales Lane
Townsend, MA 01469

KFI
35 Debevoise Ave.
Roosevelt, NY 11575

KARABELLA YARNS
1201 Broadway
New York, NY 10001

KOIGU WOOL DESIGNS
RR#1
Williamsford, ON
N0H 2V0 Canada

LBUSA
PO Box 217
Colorado Springs, CO 80903

LE FIBRE NOBILI
distributed by
Plymouth Yarn

LION BRAND YARN CO.
34 West 15th Street
New York, NY 10011

NATURALLY
distributed by
S. R. Kertzer, Ltd.

NORO YARNS
distributed by
KFI

PATON® YARNS
PO Box 40
Listowel, ON
N4W3H3 Canada

PLYMOUTH YARN
PO Box 28
Bristol, PA 19007

ROWAN YARNS
4 Townsend West, Unit #8
Nashua, NH 03063

S. R. KERTZER LTD.
105 A Winges Road
Woodbridge, ON
L4L 6C2 Canada

SESIA
distributed by
LBUSA

**SKACEL COLLECTION,
INC.**
PO Box 88110
Seattle, WA 98138-2110

STAHL WOLLE
distributed by
Skacel Collection, Inc.

TAHKI YARNS
distributed by
Glendale, NY 11385

**TAHKI·STACY CHARLES,
INC.**
8000 Cooper Ave.
Brooklyn, NY 11222

TRENDSETTER YARNS
16742 Stagg Street
Suite 104
Van Nuys, CA 91406

UNIQUE KOLOURS
1428 Oak Lane
Downingtown, PA 19335

CANADIAN RESOURCES

Write to US resources for mail-order availability of yarns not listed.

BERROCO, INC.
distributed by
S. R. Kertzer, Ltd.

CLASSIC ELITE YARNS
distributed by
S. R. Kertzer, Ltd.

DIAMOND YARN
9697 St. Laurent
Montreal, PQ H3L 2N1
and
155 Martin Ross, Unit #3
Toronto, ON M3J 2L9

NATURALLY
distributed by
S. R. Kertzer, Ltd.

PATONS ®
PO Box 40
Listowel, ON N4W 3H3

ROWAN
distributed by
Diamond Yarn

S. R. KERTZER, LTD.
105A Winges Rd.
Woodbridge, ON L4L 6C2

UK RESOURCES

Not all yarns used in this book are available in the UK. For yarns not available, make a comparable substitute or contact the US manufacturer for purchasing and mail-order information.

ROWAN YARNS
Green Lane Mill
Holmfirth
West Yorks HD7 1RW
Tel: 01484-681881

SILKSTONE
12 Market Place
Cockermouth
Cumbria, CA13 9NQ
Tel: 01900-821052

THOMAS RAMSDEN GROUP
Netherfield Road
Guiseley
West Yorks LS20 9PD
Tel: 01943-872264

VOGUE KNITTING BABY BLANKETS TWO

Editorial Director
TRISHA MALCOLM

Yarn Editor
VERONICA MANNO

Art Director
CHI LING MOY

Assistant Editor
MIRIAM GOLD

Executive Editor
CARLA S. SCOTT

Production Manager
DAVID JOINNIDES

Book Manager
MICHELLE LO

Photography
QUENET STUDIOS

Graphic Designer
CAROLINE WONG

Photo Stylist
LAURA MAFFEO

Instructions Editor
GAYLE BUNN

President, Sixth&Spring Books
ART JOINNIDES

LOOK FOR THESE OTHER TITLES IN THE *VOGUE KNITTING ON THE GO!* SERIES...